# THE ASCENT

## A JOURNEY ABOVE CANCER

BY ALEXANDRIA QUINN

*"This book is dedicated to those who need to read it; to those who are facing their own internal mountains; to those who find themselves in need of a helpful guide."*

**Alexandria Quinn**

# Prologue

It takes a particular disposition to climb a mountain; such challenges require more than just physical strength and endurance. They require a strong mind and endless determination that only a select few possess. Mountains are not made for the faint-hearted. They were formed only for the brave; for those willing to scale their enormous heights, readily placing their lives in the mountain's grasp and not knowing if they'll return, dead or alive.

My fascination with mountains began long before cancer. It began when my husband and I spontaneously booked a trip to Everest base camp. Everest had been a lifelong dream of his despite having no previous mountaineering experience. I, however, took a little more convincing before I would agree to such an enormous challenge – let's face it, it isn't your average holiday goals! But the trip was eventually sold to me. When I heard of the spiritual enlightenment that awaits in the presence of the highest point on earth, such an experience enticed me. I had spent a lifetime waiting for my big awakening. Maybe on Everest I would find the answers I was seeking.

In the end I became more obsessed with Everest than my husband. I threw myself into base camp training, whether it was timed hikes up my nearest mountains or gruelling workouts in the gym. I dedicated my time to becoming the best and fittest version of myself. Determined to complete the trip without issue, Everest soon became the centre of my life's focus. It bewitched my soul, and I put everything I had into reaching its alluring heights.

I was in the best shape of my life: strong, fit, and healthy – except that I wasn't. Just months before we were due to embark on the biggest venture of our lives I heard those dreaded words: *'I'm sorry, it's cancer.'* Surely it was a mistake?

I couldn't have cancer – I was about to climb Everest! Well, to base camp, at least. My denial was understandable. I had forced my body beyond its limits and it had prevailed. Now, all of a sudden, it failed me. I felt cheated, let down and betrayed, with no choice but to stand before a new mountain – one I had never expected to climb. A mountain more deadly than Everest herself.

I stood paralysed at its cancerous base gazing up at its monstrous heights wondering if I was brave enough to make my ascent and strong enough to make it down alive.

# Part 1

*Fortune really does favour the brave.*
*Be brave.*
*Take risks.*
*Live your life.*
*Smile.*
*And don't forget to look UP.*

**Ben Fogle, UP**

Chapter 1

# -First Steps-

I've been climbing mountains my whole life, long before I ever laid eyes on them.

My journey to the top begins and ends in Belfast. It was summer 1991, and it was raining (it always rains here). But raining or not, nothing could dampen this day. This day was special. It was the day my parents were expecting their first child together – me.

My mum had been rushed into the old maternity ward at the City Hospital with my dad accompanying her in the ambulance. Mum, aged twenty-three, was in her prime, and excited to be adding a baby girl to her small family unit. Dad, much older at forty-six, delighted in being a first-time parent; still unable to comprehend that he was finally going to be a father. My older brother, Matthew, was waiting at home with our granny and had already decided he didn't want a baby sister. But that didn't last too long.

Although we were a small family, we were a close one. Better still, we were unique. My brother and I were blessed to have parents from opposite ends of the world, which was reflected in our very different upbringing, cultural and otherwise. Dad was born and raised in Egypt and Mum grew up in Northern Ireland. Worlds apart, yet each with their own difficulties.

My dad's life began in the Mediterranean port city of Alexandria (الإسكندرية), the city from which I inherited my name and had a chance to visit in my early twenties. Alexandria is a quiet coastal refuge and popular holiday spot for many Egyptian families, but unfortunately when Dad was young house prices were high in this upmarket area and when his parents fell into financial difficulty they were forced to sell their beautiful villa by the sea and move to Egypt's busy and chaotic capital, Cairo.

Cairo is a fascinating city. No matter how many times I visit, it still continues to blow my mind. It's the largest city in the Arab world with a population of over twenty million, and is a city where the rich are rich and the poor are poor. There is no in between; it's a city split in two. Not because of religion or political beliefs, but divided by poverty. The poorer areas remain hugely overpopulated with families living on top of each other in a labyrinth of dingy alleyways and mountainous waste piles, while the richer half of society live in newly built luxury accommodation in safe, gated communities.

Regrettably my dad and his family lived among the poor in a two-bedroom apartment in the heart of the city centre. My grandparents, my three aunties and my dad (the only boy) were crammed together under one tiny roof. Yet, despite their cramped living conditions, they were happy. The family's financial strain, however, was eventually passed onto the children, forcing my dad's older sister, Samia, to give up her dream of attending university and becoming a journalist, and instead head straight to work when she finished school at 16. Unlike the UK, education is a privilege in Egypt; its doors only open for the wealthy.

Conscription in Egypt is another reason why many young Egyptians are deprived of further education. Men aged eighteen to thirty must enlist in military service and they can choose to do it before or after third-level education – if they want to continue their education, of course. If they choose to attend university first, they must complete their service after achieving their degree, which isn't overly enticing, not by that stage anyway. Exemptions from the military are only granted on medical grounds, and, luckily for my dad, he was exempt because of his flat feet (a feature I inherited), which deemed him a useless runner. But Dad wasn't disappointed.

He knew that education, not the army, was his pathway out of poverty, so, against his father's wishes, he enrolled in law school. Determined to secure a career that allowed him to leave Egypt and its poverty-stricken land behind for good.

I know very little about my dad's early years because sadly his childhood was something he never got the chance to share with me. My version of his history was actually gathered from my older cousin, Amir. He and my dad were exceptionally close, so I naturally turned to him to fill in the blanks for me. A lot of what Amir shared came as a huge surprise, especially when I learnt that my dad left law school, quitting after his first year. I had always believed my father was a decisive man, that he had his entire life figured out from the get-go – unlike myself who had no clue what to do when I left school. Turns out we're more alike than I thought.

After quitting law school my father found employment as a waiter in the Cairo Tower, a revolving restaurant offering panoramic views of the wonderous city. Dad enjoyed the work and quickly recognised the opportunities for progression, so he enrolled in catering college. A smart move. Over the next four years he excelled in his studies and earned himself an international work permit to London, succeeding in finding his one-way ticket out of Egypt.

My dad's tenacity, determination and success are traits I value immensely; traits I would one day realise I possess myself – after I found out I had cancer. My dad was living proof that anything is possible. If you set your mind to it and work hard for it, you can achieve your dreams. He was a man admired by many, a man highly respected, and a man I adored. There is no greater hero in my eyes than my beloved father.

My mum's childhood was equally as challenging but under much different circumstances. She was born into a period of violence and fear during the height of the Troubles. Northern Ireland, just like Egypt, was a divided nation ruled by politics and paramilitaries.

Belfast, like many Northern Irish cities, was a battleground between Catholics and Protestants and state forces. My mum was raised in the heart of the conflict – the Shankill Road. A proud Protestant area that borders a proud Catholic one – the Falls. Both areas suffered tragic losses at a time when bomb explosions, open gunfire, protests and murder were part of everyday life.

When I later asked my mum if she afraid growing up in the Troubles, she answered, *'No, it was just part of everyday life.'* To her, the brutality and violence was normal, which saddens me greatly. As an outsider looking in, I can see the damage such an upbringing has had on my mother and the whole population of Northern Ireland; especially the negative impact it has had on the nation's mental well-being, which I have witnessed first-hand working as a mental health nurse in Belfast. Is it any wonder Northern Ireland has the highest suicide rate in the UK, or that alcohol and drug abuse is at an all-time high?

It certainly wasn't normal when Mum's grandad was tragically blown to pieces in a bomb explosion meant for someone else while taking his evening bath, or for her brother's stepdaughter to lose her life at the age of thirteen after a bomb went off in the local fish shop. Just another child who lost her life in a conflict she was barely old enough to understand. Nor was it normal for my dear uncle to pull her lifeless body out of the rubble, a memory that haunted him for the rest of his life and that drove him to excessive drinking and an early grave. The horrors of the Troubles were certainly far from normal, but for those who lived and breathed them they were sadly *'just part of everyday life.'*

After finishing secondary school, my mum decided to try out a career in modelling. She was a slim and attractive young woman who fitted the job description perfectly, but she was unimpressed with the falseness of the industry and decided to seek out a different line of work instead. After a few temping jobs, she took on waitressing in the Europa Hotel – the hotel where my dad just so happened to be general manager. And so their love story began. A few whirlwind years later and here they were in the City Hospital awaiting the arrival of their baby girl, me.

* * *

Our family didn't remain in Belfast for long because in 1993 my dad was offered an exciting business opportunity overseas managing a new corporate hotel. Situated in the north-west of England, on Blackpool's famous promenade, was the Imperial Hotel. It didn't take my parents much convincing to leave Belfast behind and start afresh. I was two and my brother was five when we moved. I know my brother missed Belfast terribly but I never gave it a second thought, not until I reached my late teens, that is. As a child, Blackpool was a playground in a whole other league. With its amusements, theme parks, donkey rides on the beach, sticks of rock, Blackpool Tower and the dazzling Blackpool Illuminations, what wasn't there to like?

My parents bought our home just outside the busy town centre, in a quieter area, a village close to the sea. Mum chose the house and everything in it, and although it was beautiful, to me it never really felt like home. It was a show house when we bought it and my mum kept it that way. The floors were cold and tiled in Mum's favourite colour, black; the glass cabinets were jam-packed with expensive ornaments that forever needed dusting and I was terrified of breaking. The house had two sitting rooms – the fancy one my parents used with a dining room attached, and a slightly less fancy one that my brother and I used. As well as those rooms, we had a breakfast room (that I don't ever recall eating breakfast in) and a study for my dad. It was the biggest house on our block; a corner house with a stunning exotic back garden filled with monkey puzzle trees and sweet-smelling jasmine. It was my mum's dream house, her pride and joy. For a long time it was a happy home, until the atmosphere inside turned as black as the cold floor tiles.

My memories of my early years are few and far between – the result of a trauma response, according to my counsellor, but what I can remember is mostly happy times: days spent at the beach with my mum; walking the illuminations with my big brother, light-up yo-yos in hand; bedtime fairy tales read to me by my sweet father;

Sunday carvery at the hotel where the staff made a fuss of the boss's children; family outings to local hotspots; regular trips to the Lake District; and weekends up in Scotland. Yes, my childhood was certainly a happy one, albeit a lonely one.

I remember being an exceptionally quiet child. I had no friends before primary school because my parents took me out of nursery before I had the chance to make any. I accidentally burned myself on a hot radiator, and although the injury was minor my parents were maybe a tad overprotective, especially my dad, and were convinced I was safer at home. The knock-on was that I was rarely around children my own age and so I failed to develop those all-important social skills that would benefit me when I was older, which probably triggered my social anxiety in later life (also according to my counsellor).

However, despite being a loner through most of primary school, my early years were certainly never dull and I never felt like I was missing out. Thanks to my dad's hefty pay cheque, I'd say my brother and I enjoyed a very privileged upbringing. We wanted for nothing – the latest toys, the best of clothes, another pet bunny rabbit (I had six in total). Anything we asked for, we got. Although we weren't spoilt children, just lucky, I guess.

We holidayed several times a year. When we weren't exploring old monasteries in France or visiting the pyramids and my grandparents in Egypt or catching up with our family in Northern Ireland, we were enjoying holidays at our timeshare in America, which my dad bought shortly after I was born. I was still in my pram on my first trip to Disney, and I was hooked from the very beginning – from the first time I laid eyes on Sleeping Beauty's castle and witnessed the Princess Parade.

During that first trip my parents bought me a Minnie Mouse teddy bear – the traditional one with the red-and-white polka-dot dress and bright yellow shoes. I named her Minnie Ha Ha, for reasons unbeknown to my adult self, and she has never left my side since.

She was a patient in hospital with me when I had my tonsils and adenoids removed. The nurses even ensured she had the correct name band on her wrist to match mine. She travelled with me on every adventure across the globe – my poor dad having to drive all the way home from the airport to retrieve her before one of our long-haul flights. She lay beside me when I cried myself to sleep, distraught with grief. She stayed hidden in my handbag as a stowaway when I slept at my first boyfriend's house. She sailed the ocean with me when I moved back across the water. She slept in between my husband and me after we were married. She remained in my arms when I had my first bout of chemotherapy. She soaked up my tears after I had my single mastectomy. Her white hands are now stained red with my blood. She knew my story long before I wrote it; seeing each chapter unfold as I lived it. A little piece of my childhood remaining with me always.

* * *

I was ten when my parents decided to buy a local shop named The Tap House. My dad wasn't keen on the new business venture, but his hotel career had unfortunately been cut short and there weren't many other options that allowed him to work so close to home. The shop was a small convenience store selling the basic essentials as well as cigarettes and alcohol. With a decent tidy flat above to rent out, the business had potential but, alas, its potential never manifested. Not for my parents anyway.

The shop made very little profit no matter how much money my parents pumped into it, no matter what new ideas they came up with to try and increase business. It just wasn't successful. Not only did it cause our family financial strain, it also meant my dad ended up working around the clock because we couldn't afford to pay more than one member of staff – Pam, who became my lifelong friend. My mum could only help out here and there after taking on full-time employment in a local restaurant to try and keep us afloat, meaning the bulk of the hours were left to my dad. The lonely fourteen-hour shifts deflated him and his spark for life and adventure soon diminished.

Our family went from a life of luxury to watching every penny, a difficult adjustment for my parents to make. My dad tried his best to keep the mounting debts hidden from me and my brother, but the growing tension and heated discussions between my parents after bedtime were hard to miss. It broke my heart to watch my dad go from a respectable businessman to what he perceived as a failure. Even at such a young age I saw how much the demotion cost him. A man without pride is a broken man, and my dad was now unfixable. Worse still, I had no idea how to help him.

I knew I was failing him. I called in with him as often as I could to try and keep him company and break up his monotonous working day. I found him asleep in a tiny armchair in the back room on more than one occasion, his head bowed in exhaustion – a sight that still haunts me to this day. I knew my father was miserable but I didn't know how to make him better. Over time I called in less and less. Now preoccupied with high school and its petty teenage dramas, I was too young and naive to fully understand my father wasn't well.

## Chapter 2

# -A Black Christmas-

It was a Saturday evening in early December and our street already looked like a Christmas movie set except for our house, which was currently the only broken bulb in the Wolsey Close light chain. But Mum finally gave in to neighbourhood peer pressure and carted the decorations down from the attic. I was delighted. After all, it wasn't officially Christmas until your tree was up, and decorating the tree was my favourite part of the holidays. Well, besides the presents, of course.

Putting the tree up was a full-day family ritual starting off with cleaning. My mum and I spent the entire morning gutting out the front room. Every surface was meticulously cleared and polished; the floors swept and mopped, at least twice; the windows gleamed from an entire bottle of white vinegar and countless newspapers. The room was finally ready. An empty shell all set to be transformed into a winter wonderland.

The afternoon was spent preparing the Christmas banquet – a selection of finger food to nibble on while decorating the tree. I was in charge of cocktail sticks that were to be threaded with a combination of tinned ham (which you would never entertain any other time of the year), cubed cheese and pickles. I popped another piece of cheese in my mouth and hummed along to the old Christmas album playing in the corner, not lifting my head until my silver tray was full. Once satisfied that I had made enough to feed the five thousand, I took a breather and glanced up at the golden swinging clock in front of me. It was almost time: my dad would be home any minute now and we could finally get started.

Just then the phone rang as if he had read my mind. I smiled knowing Dad's persistent ring, but my smile quickly fled as I watched the phone slide from my mum's shaking hands and the colour drain from her face. She let out a muffled cry that I couldn't quite understand, but my brother had. I heard him bound down the stairs looking frightened, which in turn frightened me. He threw me my coat and ushered me out the door, the three of us heading up the street to The Tap House.

I arrived at the shop first but the uniformed men wouldn't let me in. My brother got there moments later and barged his way through with force. Mum stood beside me catching her breath, her pale face now glowing red in the cold, frosty air. The men in uniform moved from the doorway to let paramedics carry out a man on a stretcher. His chest was bare and had two white pads attached to it, and an oxygen mask covered his face. I could see no sign of movement on the stretcher. My brother walked slowly behind, his head bowed low to hide his tears. The ambulance doors slammed shut, the blue lights flickered on, the sirens started wailing, and that was the last time I ever saw my father alive. He died in the back of the ambulance that cold December night at the young age of fifty-eight. The coroner's report concluded it was a heart attack. Mum blamed her husband's early death on his unhealthy smoking habit, and I blamed his death on her and that damn shop.

I said my goodbyes to my father in the funeral home three days later; a goodbye that has stayed with me. Even now when I close my eyes I can still see the ice glistening on the footpath below my tiny feet; I can feel the cold bursts of wind cutting through my much younger face; I can replay the morbid glow of the Christmas lights in the funeral parlour windows, dancing away to their sorry tune; I can smell the distinct smell of death that lingers throughout the building – a smell that still makes my stomach retch.

My brother was the first to enter the room where my father lay, closing the door behind him; not wanting us to see him raise my father's lifeless body into his arms to cradle him one last time. Mum and I went in together for moral support. I approached the coffin with caution, afraid of what I'd find inside. I cast my eyes over my father. He was dressed in his finest navy pinstriped suit, carefully chosen by my mother. In death a proud boss again. I placed his stony slender hands in mine and kissed them ever so softly, afraid they would crack beneath my lips, and whispered my final goodbye.

A week after my father's funeral I was found lying in an deserted field covered in my own vomit, an empty vodka bottle beside me. I could hear the distant panicked voices of my friends phoning for an ambulance before the sky went blurry and I blacked out. I woke in a moving vehicle with a strange man standing over me. I recognised the uniform – I had seen it before, quite recently. I felt something sticking to my chest and peered down at the familiar white pads attached to my chest, the same ones I'd seen on my father. I heard the sirens squealing, the same sirens I'd heard the night my entire world ended. I closed my eyes willing it all to be over, to be reunited with my beloved father and escape my inconsolable grief.

Instead, I woke in a hospital bed a few hours later, bursting into tears knowing I'd been so close; so close to seeing him again and then had the opportunity snatched away. Instead of my beautiful father's angelic face I saw my mother's angry one coming towards me. I quickly closed my eyes, pretending to be asleep a little longer. Alas, feigning sleep could only delay the inevitable reprimand a short while. After my scolding a doctor came to assess my mental state. He barely gave me five minutes before determining I was only another self-destructive naughty teenager and sent me on my merry way, just in time for my morning paper round that my mum still made me do – even with twigs and vomit matted in my hair.

From the day we lost my father my relationship with my mother became a turbulent one. I wasn't the only one to turn to alcohol for consolation. Mum drank heavily too and wasn't the nicest person with drink on board.

Of course, I didn't know it then but my mum was using alcohol to escape her grief too. I never put myself in her shoes. I never acknowledged that she was now a young widow with two teenage kids to raise alone. My father's death wasn't spoken of in our house; it was a forbidden topic that was only ever mentioned during alcohol-fuelled rows. Neither of us sought grief counsellors or outside help. Instead, we developed our own unhealthy coping mechanisms; unhealthy habits that only pushed our family further apart.

For years after my father's death my mother refused to put up a Christmas tree. Once she remarried, she took herself off for the holidays; never wanting to spend them at home. I spent my Christmases either at friends' houses or with my brother and his partner Sophie. When I moved into my own house I bought a black Christmas tree that I put up every 3 December, on the anniversary of my father's death. A morbid ritual that I carried on in his honour. Until I got cancer, that is.

* * *

I've always found myself drawn to confident women. Brave women who aren't afraid to speak their minds; women who are assertive, respected and desired; women who own the room without breaking a sweat; women who own themselves. Women who are the total opposite of me.

After my father's death I was more lost than ever when, by some miracle, I fell in with one of these confident females who offered me a helping hand. Her name was Kelly. Kelly lived a few doors from our dreaded shop and just so happened to stop me one morning to pass on her family's condolences. I was surprised by the kind gesture. Kelly was one of the popular kids at school and I was unaware she knew I existed, but for some unbeknown reason, on that particular day, she decided to befriend me, and my life drastically changed. Again.

Suddenly I was popular. People actually liked me, which was so alien I couldn't accept it at first – after all, I'd spent most of my life invisible. How come people could see me now? Desperate to fit in with my new friends, I moulded myself into someone I wasn't. I wore heavy make-up, rolled my skirt up way above the knee, started smoking, acted the maggot in class, disrupted lessons, was rude to my teachers, made fun of girls who were invisible, like I used to be. It wasn't that I fell in with a bad crowd, because they weren't – they were good kids. I was the bad one.

My grades started slipping. I was no longer the A* student my dad had been so proud of. I was downgraded classes, no longer smart enough to keep up with the top set in maths, English and science. In fact, I was predicted to fail every one of my GCSEs. Not that I cared at the time.

I started drinking heavily at the weekends, often making a fool of myself or accidentally hurting myself under the influence of alcohol. I got so drunk one night that I fell and smashed my face off a kerb, knocking my front tooth out and busting my lip clean open. Worse still, I was that intoxicated I didn't even know I'd done it until I saw my bloody reflection in the mirror. I was out of control. I lost my dignity and my virginity all in one go and I was ashamed. And the more ashamed I was, the more I drank to forget the shame, and so the cycle continued.

Mum tried putting me under house arrest, permanently grounding me, but I always talked my way to freedom eventually. My teachers pleaded with me to end my reckless behaviour, so I stopped going to school. My brother slapped me out of utter frustration after I was suspended for the second time that year, so I retaliated by yelling *'You're not my real brother',* succeeding in hurting him the only way I knew how. I went from grade A student to grade A idiot, and that's putting it politely. What can I say other than I was a messed-up kid who missed her father and was pissed off at everything and everyone for taking him from her?

After another heated row with my mum I decided to live with my brother for a while to give us both some space. He had moved into the flat above our hateful shop and allowed me to crash there for a while. His living room was now my bedroom; his sofa now my bed. I was mistaken in thinking he would give me an easy ride. Instead, he laid down the ground rules immediately. Rules I now had no choice but to obey if I wanted to keep a roof over my head. My brother and I made a deal: I attended school every day, did my homework every evening, only drank when I was in his company (where my behaviour could be monitored) and was only allowed to sleep over at Kelly's house, a few doors down from him.

It meant no more bunking off school or falling behind with my schoolwork. No staying out at random house parties or drinking in the streets. As unfair as it sounds to any ASBO teenager, this strict set of rules was the kindest thing my brother could have done for me. I didn't mind my new restrictions and enjoyed my brother's and Sophie's company. They treated me like a daughter and I had a place to call home. However, the move didn't come without sacrifice.

After I moved into the flat my relationship with Kelly simmered, mainly because I wasn't able to attend the same social gatherings as she was any more. She soon chummed up with another girlfriend and I was naturally left behind, which hurt at the time – quite a lot actually. I felt betrayed by my best friend, especially when I lost more than just Kelly. I also lost her family, who I had been incredibly close with too. But such is life. Not all friendships are meant to go the distance, as I have learnt the hard way. Kelly continued to filter in and out of my life over the years. She visited me in Belfast, she came to my wedding reception, she got in touch after cancer, but then disappeared by the end of chemo. I'm not angry with her, though. Like I said, not all friendships are meant to go the distance.

Miraculously I managed to pass all my GCSEs, thanks to my brother, I suppose. I even managed to get an A* in art. After school ended and it was time to apply for colleges, I made sure I chose a different one from my old school friends. I was ashamed of my behaviour in high school and I desperately wanted to get rid of that version of myself.
College offered me that – the chance to start afresh, away from anyone who knew me before. A chance to recreate myself.

I chose to study business studies and travel and tourism at A level. Not because I wanted to, but because I thought my dad would have wanted me to. I had no idea what I wanted to do with my life other than wanting to travel, but I felt my life and career needed to live up to the same high standards as his. Going travelling certainly wouldn't suffice. I wasn't aware back then that my life didn't need to replicate my father's for it to be meaningful.

Unfortunately the subjects I chose were harder than I anticipated and left me doubting my academic capabilities. No matter how hard I tried I just couldn't keep up, especially in business studies. It went straight over my head and I knew I would never pass my exams. As usual, I struggled to make new friends. Without a confident female by my side I had no voice. I was invisible again and I was embarrassed by it. Eventually I convinced myself I wasn't smart enough to study A levels and wasn't going to put myself through another year of social awkwardness, so I quit. I finished my first-year exams, dropped my pen on the paper, walked out of the exam hall and never looked back.

Quitting college was the first decision I ever made for myself. It was impulsive and scary but I chose to do it. No one influenced my decision, just me. It felt right for me at the time, even if it did make me feel like a failure. I had no plan, no idea of what to do next, but I quit anyway. Maybe some journeys aren't meant to be straightforward. Mine certainly wasn't.

* * *

I was working in an upholstery business when I came across an ad for an apprenticeship at a local nursery. At the time I was employed by my mum's new husband, John, and as much as I was grateful for the work and the more than decent pay cheque, I was totally useless at the job. I oversaw front of house, answering the phone and helping customers who called into the store. Most orders were placed over the phone or computer, thankfully sparing me the embarrassment of pretending I knew about fabrics and furniture. The work was lonely and, to put it kindly, boring.

The furniture was made in the factory behind the reception and I preferred to keep the door between the two firmly closed. The factory lads all knew I was useless and that I'd only been hired because the boss had a new missus. The less interaction with them the better. It was not a job for an eighteen-year-old. There were no opportunities to make new friends or progress in a career, and there was certainly no craic at the office. Well, not on my side of the door anyway.

Although I was thankful for the favour from John, I was understandably bored stiff, so I applied for the apprenticeship. Not because I was overly passionate about working with young children, but because it offered something better than my current situation. As well as a recognised qualification in childcare, there was the chance to mingle with girls my own age and a chance to build a new life again.

The nursery was segregated into three parts: a baby unit, two and three year olds, and preschool. I was luckily allocated the two and three year olds because babies weren't really my forte, to be honest – not then anyway. Toddlers are much more entertaining

– so mischievous at that age it was comical. Of course I'd have probably found it much less amusing if they were my children, but they weren't, which was the beauty of the job. Nursery routine was simple and easy to follow, meaning that for once I didn't feel stupid or out of my depth. I felt relaxed there and made a few lifelong friends, one being Chloe.

Surprisingly, I had known Chloe most of my life. Our brothers had grown up together and were very close, but Chloe and I had remained strangers until now. We had never exchanged more than a polite hello prior to working together.
We were polar opposites, yet the perfect match. She was loud and bubbly – a girl who oozed confidence; whereas I was quiet, withdrawn and massively uncomfortable in my own skin. She was a girly girl and I was a tomboy. Even our favourite colours clashed: hers pink and mine a morbid black. She was open and wore her heart on her sleeve; I was a closed book, allowing only a select few to read past my first chapter. I suppose I was the dark and she was the light, and somehow we just clicked somewhere in the middle.

When I was with Chloe I felt confident, just like I had with Kelly, and just as before I fed and thrived on that false confidence knowing I couldn't survive without it. For a while we were inseparable and did everything together, rarely going a day without seeing each other. During one of our standard movie nights, that usually occurred when we were too hungover to do anything else, Chloe and I decided to watch Eat Pray Love. Julia Roberts plays Liz, a journalist, who shares my passion for travel, and luckily for her makes a living out of it. Outside of her jet-set lifestyle, though, the rest of her world is crumbling. She is married to a man she no longer loves, lives in a beautiful home she designed herself but no longer feels part of and has become a woman without purpose, without faith, without an appetite for life. A woman *'without a pulse.'*

The film follows Liz as she falls apart after filing for divorce and losing everything she owns. Hoping to remember how to eat, pray and love, she embarks on a journey of self-discovery starting in Italy, travels on to a guru meditation camp in India and finally finishes in Bali. During her travels Liz learns to eat again, and by replenishing her appetite for food she rediscovers her appetite for life. She learns to pray through the art of meditation, allowing her to successfully restore her balance and feel content with life once more. Finally Liz learns to love again when she meets a hot Australian man in Bali, and quite literally sails off into the sunset with him!

By the end of the film Chloe and I were both in tears and thinking the exact same thing: OMG, Alex, you are Liz! Not because I'm a Julia Roberts lookalike (I wish) or that I wanted to leave my non-existent husband, but because I was lost and needed to find myself again, just as Liz had. From that day forth I became obsessed with my own journey of self-discovery. I wanted to travel to Italy, India and Bali and recreate my own version of the film and get my happily ever after. Chloe, of course, agreed to come with me, and we spent hours locked away in my bedroom hypothetically planning our big escape.

Although we talked about it like it was our dream I always knew it was mine, not hers. Chloe, like most young women, wanted to get married, have a big family and settle down in her home town close to her family and friends. Whereas I had no desire to remain in Blackpool, nor did I desire the conventional lifestyle. I wanted more. Realistically I'd been craving an escape from Blackpool ever since my dad died, and after watching my now favourite movie my mind was made up. Eat Pray Love only confirmed what I already knew: that I didn't belong here, that I was destined for something else; something bigger than Blackpool, something bigger than me.

But several years passed without change. I was still stuck in the same miserable seaside town no closer to catching that dream flight as I was when the idea first came to mind. Chloe, however, had found her movie ending. She had settled down and was in a serious relationship, like all my friends were now. Although I was delighted she had found her special someone, I missed the good old days when it was just the two of us against the world – usually drunk in our local pub!

Even though Chloe tried her best to include me in her new life, I knew I had to take a back seat and let her live hers while I tried to figure out mine. I had to accept that my closest friend and I had reached a crossroads. With a heavy heart, she went her way and I went mine.

## Chapter 3

# -Appearances Can Be Deceiving-

A mountain's appearance can often be deceiving. You can start your ascent in the brilliant sunshine without a single cloud in the sky, yet when you reach the summit you can be greeted with turbulent winds, pelting rain or thick dense fog. Mountaineers must, therefore, be prepared to encounter all climbing conditions when they make their ascent. Just as a mountain's appearance can play tricks on you, so did mine. On the outside I was a relatively *'normal'* young women entering her twenties, but on the inside I was screaming.

Like many young women I found my insecurities overbearing. Being single was just one of them – as if being single was the worst thing in the world. I felt this desperate need to be in a relationship, like all my friends were, so that I could be *'normal.'* To me, being single automatically made me an outcast because I was completely alone. Like so many, I believed we humans are destined to partner up with someone – as if our sole purpose in life is to pair with another. But what if that's not the case?

It's a shame that so many of us feel forced into relationships we often don't want to be in just to be accepted among our peers. Even worse, society has now added a timescale in which we must find this significant other. Nowadays if you're not married by thirty or at least have a ring on your finger, you're classed as some sort of reject, which is ludicrous. Surely there's no timeframe for love? Or what if you don't feel the need to conform to society's unrealistic expectations? What if you're perfectly happy going alone at this thing called life? If I'd have been braver, I'd have done just that. I'd have given relationships a miss for a while and chose adventure over love – because adventure was my love, back then, at least.

But I wasn't brave enough to just be me, to just go for it and live my life exactly the way I wanted. Instead, I chose to be like everyone else, and, in turn, I rejected my true self.

I went through numerous pointless relationships, one after the other, believing I was in love every time. But my relationships never lasted longer than six months and I was always the one getting binned, not the other way round. I dated your stereotypical potheads – guys who love cannabis more than they can ever love a woman. Men – or should I say boys, whom I had absolutely nothing in common with; men who lacked ambition, passion or any kind of drive. Those who did possess such qualities, soon realised they didn't want me in the picture. I was hardly an attractive person myself, either in looks or personality.

I came close to love only once before meeting my husband. He was older than me, one of my brother's close friends. He was my schoolgirl crush – the type of crush you're always awkward and embarrassing around. I'd get my words muddled up whenever he tried to speak to me, or clumsily spill drinks everywhere when he was about, or drink too much and make an idiot of myself as usual. He always seemed to catch me at my worst. There was no way he could ever fancy a girl like me, although we did share a few common interests. The main one being we both wanted to leave Blackpool. He wanted to emigrate to Thailand, and he filled my head with visions of living a free life in South East Asia. I dreamt he would take me with him and we would live happily ever after in a bamboo house with no electricity in the middle of the rainforest, like Tarzan and Jane. Yes, I was a hopeless romantic back then and a hopeless fool.

Years went by and we both dated other people but I always had a soft spot in my heart for him until one night I drunkenly confessed my feelings. Relying on alcohol to give me false courage and waiting for his instant rejection, I was pleasantly surprised when he didn't laugh in my face and promptly knock me down.

Instead, he agreed to give us a go. Sadly Tarzan and Jane just weren't meant to be, though. We had only been dating a few short weeks when he suddenly decided to end it. I never really understood his reasons why. His rejection without a valid reason left me understandably hurt, and I never really forgave him for that.

As I hit my early twenties I started to believe that my bad luck with men was all down to two things: my weight and my unnatural body hair. I was a curvy girl, a typical pear shape – small boobs, big hips and a large round bum. I wasn't overweight – in actual fact I was one of the smaller girls in my group of friends, yet I genuinely believed I was the heaviest. I was obsessed with how my body looked. I hated my chunky thighs, childbearing hips and oversized ass. I followed all the latest fad diets: the juice diet, the Atkins diet, SlimFast. I'd substitute juices for meals, or milkshakes for meals, or tasteless cardboard chewy bars that were meant to be a treat for snacks. I'd starve myself all week only to binge at the weekends, consequently ruining my weekday efforts. I didn't know how to lose weight healthily or how to exercise properly. I hated gyms and avoided them like the plague, always too conscious that people would be looking at me (like most gym phobics believe). I watched exercise DVDs at home instead, usually from the latest celebrity in the spotlight who had achieved a remarkable body transformation. I didn't take into consideration that these celebrities most likely had their own nutritionist, personal chef and personal trainers, or that most of them ended up piling the weight back on shortly after because their weight loss was unsustainable. I just saw a skinny celebrity on a DVD cover and thought I'd magically look like them too.

Unlike my friends who were all super confident, I was super self-critical and preoccupied with my outward appearance, especially my abnormal body hair, which was possibly a result of my Egyptian heritage. It started when I hit puberty, and naturally I was teased in school because of the unfeminine body hair that covered my legs and arms, and my hairy top lip and monobrow. The boys would made monkey noises behind my back, until one day I stole my mum's razor and shaved everything – including my forearms and top lip, which aren't supposed to be shaved and tend to grow back worse! It worked, though. Once I was hair free the boys soon stopped referring to me as a zoo animal. But the damage, of course, was already done. From that moment on I was tormented with an unhealthy hair-removal obsession. Well, until I had my breast cut off and realised there are worse things than hairy legs and a subtle moustache.

Years passed before I heard that my unnatural hair growth could have been down to medical issues, not my Egyptian blood. A treatable hormone imbalance, for example, could be the cause. Up to ten per cent of women are affected with this imbalance, known as hirsutism – hair growth in a typical male pattern meaning you get hair where most women don't because of high levels of male sex hormones. Successful treatments include oral contraception used to regulate the function of the ovaries and reduce the number of androgens they secrete, as well as laser hair removal provided on the NHS. Damn it! I was never offered either treatment because I never confided in a doctor. Instead, I let my body hair rule my life. It controlled what I wore, when I went out, when I went on holiday, when I had sex. For a long time it controlled my entire existence.

If only I had known that in less than ten years' time I would be diagnosed with cancer, oh, how I would have done things differently – treated myself differently, lived my life differently. If I had been able to predict the future and understood that I was living on borrowed time, I wouldn't have wasted so many years hating myself and often wishing my life was over already. I took the promise of tomorrow for granted. I didn't understand how precious my years were. Consumed with insecurity and self-hate, I wasted years merely existing without actually living.

So when death arrived at my door, to take me far too young, I couldn't help thinking – had I brought death upon myself?

* * *

If I could choose one word to describe my early twenties, it would be *'lonely.'* Everyone I cared about had successfully entered adulthood, bought their first homes, had children, got married. But I was still single, childless and living at my mum's house. I spent most of my time either working or drinking myself into oblivion. My life was going nowhere fast and I felt powerless to change it. My drinking increased and my self-loathing grew intolerable.

I soon found I was only able to socialise with alcohol on board. I was so anxious without it I couldn't walk into a room by myself. I couldn't attend birthday parties or other social gatherings without already being inebriated. I could barely even make it to Asda without having a panic attack and feeling like everyone was looking at me. My anxiety ate away at me and eventually I started avoiding situations that provoked it, which was pretty much everything other than work. I spent most of my time alone. I withdrew from my friends and family, feeling like a burden to them all. I didn't want to ruin their happiness.

Both my mum and brother had moved on with their lives and left the family home. Mum had remarried and was living in the Lake District. My brother had his own place too and was now a father, and I was left to roam our once happy home alone. It was nobody's fault. I couldn't be angry or upset with anyone. Everyone had the right to enjoy their lives. No one could have helped the fact that I hated mine.

It was the saddest and unhappiest time of my life. I felt like I had no one to turn to, no way out. I found that the more time I spent alone the less I wanted to see people. I couldn't bear to admit that I was depressed and refused to seek professional help. Intrusive thoughts tortured my mind constantly. I began imagining myself crashing my car into a tree or taking tablets and drifting off to sleep forever, which I tried once but messed that up too. As soon as I'd swallowed the last paracetamol and realised what I'd done, I phoned my brother crying hysterically. He brought me straight to hospital to have my stomach pumped, and I got to listen to insensitive nurses repeating to one another that *'I was a waste of a bed',* which I probably was. Truth was, I didn't want to die; I just didn't want to live. Not my life anyway. If I could have hopped into someone else's, I'd have been more than happy, but of course that wasn't an option.

During that overnight hospital stint, in my hospital gown and hospital bed, I knew I needed to make some drastic changes if I ever wanted to see a future. Only a few months later I mustered the courage, took a huge leap of faith and set myself free.

After a long and very emotional phone call with my granny in Northern Ireland, I booked a one-way ferry ticket and moved home.

Back to Belfast. Back to where I belonged.

* * *

Before I could leave my old home for good, however, I wanted to ensure I was on good terms with everyone I was leaving behind, including my mother. Our relationship was still very turbulent and I wanted to try and resolve that before I left, for both our sakes. We talked and agreed to book a trip to Egypt together, departing the month before I planned to leave England. It would seem both my motherlands were calling me home: Egypt and Northern Ireland. I had to visit them both to start afresh. Although we had visited Egypt regularly when I was child, none of my family had ventured back there since the death of my father.

Just like us, the country had evolved and changed, for the better and for the worse.

Tourism had taken over the Third World country, which was a good thing for many as it brought in revenue and provided jobs for Egypt's ever-growing population. But for me tourism had stolen a little piece of Egypt's heart. When we landed in Cairo I saw how the opportunity to make money had sliced into the once vast desert to make room for expensive hotel resorts directly facing the pyramids. Now these enormous shrines and temples faced the latest five-star hotel and spa; their authenticity stolen by tourism, their magic minimised by commercialism.

We travelled further south, making our way to Luxor and the Valley of the Kings. During the journey I found myself thinking of my beloved father more than ever. Wondering what his life had been like when he lived here, before I knew him. I felt close to him there, in Egypt. I felt that connection I'd been chasing ever since his death. I felt his presence from the moment I stepped off the plane and it comforted me. I was in a state of limbo soon to embark on the biggest adventure of my life, and I needed his guidance now more than ever.

Mum and I had chosen to take a Nile cruise, a lifelong dream for both of us. Sailing from Luxor to Aswan, the cruise would take us through some of Egypt's greatest wonders. I'd never cruised before and found it surprisingly enjoyable. The stillness of the river gave me a chance to quiet my mind. Time seemed to stand still along this river of secrets, allowing Mum and me to take the time to finally talk. We bonded along that journey, opening up to one another after years of silence. The trip was a success and I was relieved. I knew I could now leave Blackpool and my family behind with no regrets.

I found a piece of me in Egypt; a part of me that I had buried long ago. I allowed myself to get lost among the rows upon rows of sandstone pillars in the 250 acres of Karnak; a city of temples and Egypt's most remarkable religious complex dedicated to Amun, Mut and Khonsu. I listened to our tour guide's explanation of the temple with high-tuned ears.

Egypt had always fascinated me, but now, as an adult, I finally understood why: it was breathtaking. It was steeped in ancient history, my own history, my heritage.

When we visited the Temple of Hatshepsut I was spellbound. Here before me was a temple dedicated to the third female pharaoh in three thousand years of ancient Egyptian history. This pharaoh and woman of great power was part of my ancestry and therefore part of me. As I wandered through her glorious temple I was ashamed to admit I had turned my back on my lineage for so long. I decided I would no longer hide who I was. I would be proud to descend from such greatness and I would be proud to be an Egyptian woman.

One of the trip's highlights, and my personal favourite, was the Temple of Philae. A temple that had been completely relocated and restored after its original location flooded. The idea that the ancient Egyptians were able to move an entire temple simply blew my mind. The ruin was successfully moved to an island only accessible by tiny boats. Dedicated to the goddess Isis, it is perhaps the most beautiful of all the Egyptian temples and one that took my breath away.

But, as fascinating as these ancient ruins were, the most significant part of the holiday for me was the Nile itself. The world's longest river and the source of Egypt's vast history. During that week-long cruise I found myself gazing out at the children playing at the water's edge waving eagerly at the boats passing by. These children had very little, and yet here they were smiling at strangers who soaked up their lands – lands that they couldn't afford to enjoy themselves. I searched the schoolboys' faces and saw my dad in each and every one of them. I watched elderly ladies rowing up beside the cruise liners on their tiny wooden row boats hoping to sell handmade goods to those on board. Giving their customers a toothless smile, they tossed silk fashion accessories to tourists on board and held their hands out for coins.

The simplicity of life along the Nile made me assess my own life and how much I now valued it. As I watched those dreamy burnt-orange sunrises and sunsets reflecting off the water's edge I reflected on my own life, wondering if I'd made the right decision to move home and questioning whether my leap of faith would actually pay off. Like the wonders of the Nile, only time would tell.

I left Egypt in a river of tears, not wanting to leave the country where I had felt such a strong connection and afraid to face the changes waiting for me when I returned home. But I had made my decision and I had to stick by it. I had to be true to myself just this once and not cave into fear.

Chapter 4

# -The Adventure Begins-

It wasn't Italy or India or Bali but rainy Northern Ireland where my adventure finally began. Situated by the sea, just outside Belfast, Bangor is a small commuter town slightly bigger than the one I left behind. Although the town isn't overly exciting, there's still a steady hustle and bustle about the place. The people are friendly and welcoming, unlike the stand-offish community I had left behind, and it seemed like the perfect starting point to build my new life. I spent most of my days down at the beach walking along the coast, exploring and soaking up the last of the summer sun. The seaside was a comfort to me, especially on the days when I was missing home, which I often did.

I had moved to Northern Ireland with nothing to my name and only my little car and limited possessions. I had no savings, no employment and no financial security. I knew no one other than my grandparents, aunties, uncle and a few cousins whom I had never really spent any quality time with. I had taken a huge gamble with my decision to move but I had a solid plan: I intended to go back to college to finish my A levels and go to university and study for a nursing degree. I figured nursing would open up new career opportunities, including working abroad. I had my eyes set on Australia as my final destination. Belfast was only a stepping stone on to a bigger journey ahead. Except I never left in the end.

The first few months were tough and I often wondered had I made a huge mistake, but my granny kept my spirits high. She welcomed me into her home, treating me like one of her own. Now that I was blessed with the company of my grandparents, I was never really alone. My granny and I would sit for hours at her kitchen table smoking and drinking endless cups of tea and coffee, setting the world to rights.

I was able to talk openly with her about why I had moved, and how desperate I was to change my life. She motivated me on my bad days, ensuring I never gave up. Miraculously I didn't, and that I owe to her.

I must have applied for fifty plus jobs in my first few weeks in Bangor. I answered every vacancy no matter what the vocation and was rejected by every single one. I never even made it to the interview stage. I was, believe it or not, rejected for charity work at the local dog shelter – people didn't even want me to work for them for free. I naturally became downhearted and constantly worried about my finances but I kept on applying, hoping something would turn up soon. In the meantime, I enrolled in college and threw myself into my studies in preparation for university.

Thankfully I only remained unemployed for two months. I found a job in a local nursing home (both my granny and aunty had worked there, which probably swayed the interview in my favour, but I wasn't about to complain. I was just happy to be earning again). Six months later I was offered my first trust post with the NHS. My new job involved working with children and young people with learning disabilities and challenging behaviour. The job was massively out of my comfort zone, especially with having no previous experience in this area, and I spent the first three months crying on my way in to work and crying on my way out. The children often became aggressive and were exceptionally difficult to manage. My colleagues and I were injured on a regular basis and the tension and stress of the environment had a huge impact on our physical and mental health. Although the job was frightening at times it was also rewarding and swayed me towards a career in mental health nursing rather than general.

Despite the unit being highly stressful, it was here I met my closest friends. There was Gillian – an angel in disguise, Jenna – my feisty feminist, Karen – my adventure buddy and Barbara – my intellectual go-to girl. Our friendships came naturally, forged in difficult situations and maintained long after we all left the job. I found myself connected to them in a different way to my girlfriends back home. I suppose we had more common ground given our chosen careers, and after finding them my transition to life in Northern Ireland was almost complete. Within a year everything had fallen into place. It's amazing what you can do when you put your mind to it. Excuse the cliché, but it's true. I finally felt like I was on the right track. Once I had removed the negativity from my life, everything seemed to run smoothly. There was only one thing I was missing: a significant other.

I joined an online dating agency – something I'd never done before but apparently it's the only way to meet guys these days. I wasn't expecting love but was hopeful for a date or two, at least. I liked the idea of hiding behind a computer screen and not having to worry about what I looked like or if the men behind the screen found me attractive or not. I could just be me. Turns out online dating never really was for me. I only went on two dates. The first one was a complete disaster. The second date was with my future husband.

* * *

Graeme and I had been chatting for a few weeks before we decided to meet. I chose the location – The Jamaica Inn, a cute restaurant situated along the seafront in Bangor, and close to home just in case Graeme turned out to be a crazy axe murderer. I had chosen to sit outside to make the most of the gorgeous sea view. Under the heaters and twinkling fairy lights, it was more romantic than I had anticipated and that made me uncomfortable. I didn't really do romance – not any more, but as far as first dates go this one couldn't have been more perfect!

I found myself attracted to Graeme instantly, drawn to his bright blue eyes and easy-going smile. He talked so confidently and seemed so relaxed, while I was a nervous wreck hiding my shaky, sweaty hands under the table. His life sounded so fresh and exciting, I let him talk, interested to hear more. He had a lot of hobbies and interests, unlike me. He was into sports, but not your usual type. He shot clay pigeons – a sport I'd never heard of until then, and had shot professionally for Northern Ireland, travelling to South Africa in his teenage years to compete. The complete opposite to my teenage years of underage drinking and reckless behaviour. Let's not mention that yet, Alex! He was a keen fisherman and had spent three weeks out in Canada on a fishing trip. All his adventures sounded fascinating. Here was a man who actually had hobbies and interests that didn't revolve around drink, drugs and partying; setting him miles apart from the boys I had dated back home. I found his uniqueness intriguing. Yes, he was a little odd and spoke with a country accent, which I struggled to understand, but I decided I liked him.

Over the next few months Graeme introduced me to his world and I fell in love with it. Every date was an adventure. I acknowledged the thought he put into each experience – it was sweet. I assumed he was trying to show off Northern Ireland in the hope that I'd want to stay, but I had no intention of going anywhere, not for a while anyway. I had made Graeme aware from the start that I still hoped to move to Australia but he was determined to convince me otherwise.

He taught me how to fish, how to shoot, how to golf, how to sail and how to make love, not just have sex. He showed me how to have fun in ways I never could have imagined. We dedicated our time to getting to know one another, taking it slow and steady. I knew his secrets and eventually he knew mine, and surprisingly he accepted them. We cared for one another deeply, and I knew this was different to any past relationship. This was something more.

But what I liked about Graeme more than anything was his determination to make me happy, his awareness of my internal sadness and how much he tried to rectify it.

I fell in love with Ireland, both north and south, and I fell in love with Graeme, the man who finally brought me back to life.

Our first holiday abroad was naturally going to be Egypt – although it had been Graeme's choice not mine, to my surprise. We had booked the trip for my twenty-fifth birthday in June and I was super excited, as I always am before a holiday. Graeme, however, was uptight and slightly off. I didn't know what his problem was but I was already getting irritated by it. He barely said a word in the airport or on the five and a half hour flight. I couldn't understand his behaviour and quite frankly it was ruining our holiday before it even began.

We arrived in Egypt after dark. The restaurant was closed but the bar was still open. We had just finished our second drink when Graeme decided he wanted to go to bed. Already? Maybe he wanted to have hot, steamy sex? Or maybe not. He got straight into bed, gave me a quick peck on the lips and rolled over. So much for a romantic holiday, hey?

The following morning we attended the standard hotel welcome meeting. Browsing through the optional activities and excursions provided by the hotel, Graeme was only interested in one activity: diving. Of course he had no interest in seeing the pyramids or any other cultural excursions. Luckily I was keen to try diving as well. It was something I'd always wanted to do, and we'd spoken about it a few times. In the end we chose a couple of trips. I wanted to make our first holiday as memorable as possible, so we booked a trip to the pyramids, a diving experience, swimming with dolphins and a day out at sea. Graeme was so keen to dive he booked it for the following day.

There were six of us in total on the dive, with two instructors there to keep us right. We were taught the techniques on the beach first and then given the opportunity to practise them in the sea. Before I knew it we were ready to dive – apparently. The oxygen tank was so heavy I could barely wade through the water. My legs were trembling and my anxiety was kicking in as always.

I started panicking and could barely remember a word the instructors said other than thumbs up meant you wanted to resurface.

Graeme was a natural, of course, as he is with all outdoor activities, and I was a disaster. I struggled to equalise under the water. My ears screamed with the pressure and I couldn't get my buoyancy under control. I was either crawling along the seabed or floating off into sea space with the instructor frantically swimming after me, grabbing my ankles and yanking me back down to safety. It was embarrassing. The other holidaymakers were managing fine, but not me. I never saw the swarms of bright orange fish circling us, or the rainbow coral dancing along the seabed. I think there may have been a shipwreck too, but I never caught sight of it either. I was completely blinded in my panic and distracted with the pain in my ears. I was not enjoying the experience. Never again! I thought.

Just when I was about to stick my thumb up and abort, the instructor spun me round. Bobbing in front of me was Graeme, and he was holding a wooden sign in his hands – why did he have a sign? What did it say? I could just about make out the writing through my steamy goggles: Will you marry me, Alexandria? I inhaled one massive gulp of air and my ears suddenly popped – thank God for that!

I was delighted and shocked with his unexpected proposal. We hadn't even mentioned the word *'marriage',* and yet here I was now engaged. I was ecstatic and terrified at the same time. We spent the next few days scouring Egyptian jewellers to pick a ring. The sentimental value of picking my ring in Egypt wasn't lost on me. My ring would come from my dad's birthplace, making it the greatest treasure of all, and was part of Graeme's decision to come to Egypt in the first place. In the end I chose a beautiful 24-carat white gold ring with a generous diamond and unusual surrounding stones. I couldn't take my eyes off it as it twinkled in the sunlight.

Now that Graeme was back to his normal self we could celebrate and enjoy Egypt. He had obviously been worried about the proposal – even though my answer was always going to be yes, but he could relax and take in Egypt for all its beauty now. He actually enjoyed the pyramids more than I did in the end. He embraced the Egyptian culture full-heartedly, which warmed my own heart even more. Sharm El Sheik will forever be our most memorable holiday for so many reasons. By the time we arrived home I still couldn't comprehend that someone loved me enough to marry me. It was the most peculiar feeling and one that I never wanted to end.

* * *

*'Why do you want to be a nurse?'* a lady in the panel of four asked me at my nursing interview at Queen's University. The most common answers I knew went along the lines of: *'I've wanted to be a nurse my whole life'* or *'I looked after my granny and grandad when I was a teenager'* or *'I'm just a caring person by nature.'* All of which may be true, but more often than not were for the benefit of the interviewer.

Obviously there is something that draws people to the field of nursing – maybe a trauma that occurred within their family, a trauma that happened to the person themselves, the nursing gene runs in their blood or they just like the security of having a job that's promised for life with a decent pension. But more often than not people choose to be a nurse because they are damaged in some way and are seeking to fix themselves.

Truth was, my decision to study mental health nursing wasn't made overnight. It was an idea that developed over several years. It began when I took on a home care job in Blackpool working with the elderly and discovered I was surprisingly good at looking after other people. Caring for others is something that comes naturally to me, more so than caring for myself.

Better still, I enjoyed the work, which was also surprising as I didn't enjoy very much back then other than drinking myself into oblivion.

Naturally I was swayed towards the field of mental health after battling my own mental demons for the majority of my life. I figured, in learning how to help others I may at long last figure out how to help myself. That was the real reason I wanted to be a nurse – because I was damaged goods and I needed to learn how to heal myself.

Of course I passed the interview with flying colours. My rehearsed response that didn't include any of the above went down a treat. Revealing my truth at that stage may have led to failure and failure was not an option. Not this time. So a few weeks later there I was standing in the queue for my first lecture at Queen's University feeling as miniscule as a mouse among an angry herd. My instinct screamed at me to turn tail and run. My palms were clammy, my heart racing, my anxiety stifling.

I was in way over my head. You can't do this, you can't do this, my inner mean girl repeated. Just as I was about to agree and make a swift exit, a young blonde turned and gave me an awkward smile, calming my nerves instantly and convincing me to stay put. The young, pretty blonde was Katie, and we clicked from day one – even more so when we discovered we both shared a passion for travel. By the end of our first lecture our hypothetical trip to Thailand was born, and over the next three years we made that trip a reality.

My friendship circle in uni was small. There was just the three of us: Katie, Georgia and me. I was six years older than them both but the age gap never really bothered me. I liked listening to their relationship dramas and scandal. It made me chuckle. After all, I had been there, done that and worn the bloody T-shirt! I liked being the older, wiser friend for a change. Being responsible was refreshing – well, at least when I was sober, anyway. Some things will never change, hey?

University wasn't quite what any of us were expecting. Our chosen career turned out to be a full-time job long before we qualified. Freshers' parties and summer holidays in Ibiza were totally out of the question. A nursing degree is a seven-day week commitment, unlike most degrees. It was the most stressful three years of our lives, and each of us had a breakdown at one point or another – sometimes on multiple occasions. The pressure was immense. As a matter of fact, it was more than immense – it was completely exhausting.

Unfortunately I had to work and study, like the majority of mature students do. I didn't have the advantage of still living with my parents. I struggled to juggle my job around placements and eventually had to give up my permanent post and work as bank staff instead. Now, bank work is great because it's flexible but it's also temporary, which means there is either loads of work available or none. To get round this, I worked like a horse when the shifts were going to finance myself through the dry spells. University very quickly became all work and no play. Between placements, lectures, exams, assignments, work and bills to worry about, it was a real struggle.

I ended up working night shift instead of days because it meant I could work and go to uni – even though this was probably illegal because there weren't enough rest hours between the two. In fact, there were no rest hours between the two. I'd go from night shift straight to lectures surviving on copious amounts of coffee and energy drinks to get me through the day. In the evening I'd crawl through my front door and collapse on the sofa in an exhausted, shaky mess. It was unhealthy but it was necessary.

I barely saw Graeme or my friends or family during uni – I just didn't have the time. And any free time was dedicated to assignments and revision, and that was my life for three long, tiresome years. The only break I got was my holidays and I lived for them.

## Chapter 5

# -Some Things Are Meant To Be-

At the end of first year I took a trip with my soon-to-be in-laws. The six of us – Graeme's parents, Andrew and Lynda, and his sister Laura and her husband Willi, jetted off for a two-week break to my parents' old timeshare in Orlando, Florida. We had a jam-packed schedule, ensuring we squeezed in everything Orlando had to offer; purposely saving my favourite park, Disney, to last. We were visiting during my favourite time of year, Halloween, and Disney were throwing their unmissable Mickey's Not-So-Scary Halloween Party.

We arrived at Disney's Magic Kingdom at 7 p.m. sharp, just after sundown. Those with day passes were just leaving as the night owls were entering. There were pumpkin displays everywhere, with over three hundred pumpkins used in Disney's Main Street windows and shopfronts alone! Even more impressive, I later read that no two pumpkins are alike as they are each carved individually by select members of the Resort Enhancement Team. The place looked incredible. Everyone was in fancy dress – entire families had come dressed in costume. I didn't know which way to look.

Andrew and Lynda had decided to sit this one out and have an evening to themselves, so it was just the four of us. We entered the park, were handed trick-or-treat bags and a map of the Halloween trail, and off we went to trick or treat around Disneyland. A dream come true. The weather was horrendous that evening, which only made the night more memorable. The rain forcefully lashed from the heavens but we didn't let it spoil the party. We bought matching Mickey Mouse raincoats and continued along the haunted trail, filling our bags with candy as we went; Laura and I in our element with the two boys traipsing along behind.

When the skies finally cleared the Sanderson Sisters took to the stage performing a tribute act to Disney's Hocus Pocus. Laura and I squeezed our way to the front of the crowd hoping for a better view of the sisters, Winnie, Sarah and Mary, and leaving the boys sitting against a gravestone looking bored already. We managed to secure the perfect spot directly in front of the stage and squealed our way through *'I Put A Spell On You'.* After the witches had finished, Mickey's Boo-To-You Parade started accompanied by Halloween music, spooky costumes, Disney villains and spooktacular dancers. Every character was dressed in costume, including Minnie Mouse. I spotted her standing on her float wearing a dark plum witch outfit waving her broomstick at the crowd, which was more than enough to make me cry – for the umpteenth time that holiday. Disneyland has a funny way of doing that to you – evoking powerful emotions intense enough to make grown adults cry. There's an innocence about the place that naturally brings people back to their childhoods; back to when make-believe was real and happily ever after really did exist. That's how I felt that evening as I stood dripping from head to toe watching the epic show dazzling before me; weeping silently to myself while reminiscing about happy memories from my childhood, back when my family was whole.

Any trip to Disneyland is a special one but this one in particular was special for me. Firstly because I was visiting Orlando as an adult this time round, meaning I could fully understand the magnitude of the theme parks, shows and events and appreciate their creativity, technology and general awesomeness. Secondly, it gave me the opportunity to bond with my in-laws, especially Laura. Although Laura and I had always been friendly, I had never considered us to be close, but after spending two weeks in the most magical place on earth I had gained far more than a friend – I had gained a sister.

It was comforting to feel valued and accepted into a family again. My own family was still a broken one, unfortunately – maybe more so now than ever. Since moving away I'd become even more alienated from both my brother and my mother. Sadly, as new family relationships blossomed, old relationships continued to wither.

I admit I had made less time for my family back home in Blackpool. I was busy creating a new life for myself, which meant I didn't prioritise my old one. Yes, that may have been selfish, but my life had taken a new direction and for once I had to put myself first. I had my own family now, a fiancé, friends, a home to run and a degree to complete. Not to mention that I didn't live just round the corner any more.

I did my best to visit when I could but there was no denying my brother and I had grown apart. I felt that he resented my new-found happiness and lifestyle that I had worked so hard to achieve. He had visited me only once in the three years since I had left home, which Graeme had arranged as a surprise for Christmas. I was delighted to spend time with him and my nephew, Ethan, over the holidays but my brother spent the entire week behaving like he didn't want to be there. He seldom contacted me after that awkward visit and never gave any reason for his strange behaviour. When I FaceTimed my nephew, my brother left the room, which made me upset and uncomfortable, so after a while I stopped communicating too – both with him and Ethan, which I knew was wrong. Ethan was just an innocent victim in our stupid sibling feud. When my brother had his second son Conor, our feud escalated beyond repair.

I delayed meeting newborn Conor until I visited for Ethan's birthday just a few months later. I felt this was justified because it meant I wouldn't have to travel over twice in such a short space of time, but my brother didn't agree – especially as I managed to squeeze in my trip to America before meeting my youngest nephew (which had been booked prior to Conor even being conceived – but that wasn't valid, apparently).

A week before Ethan's birthday a horrible argument blew up between my brother and me – one that had been brewing for months, I guess. After almost a year of silence neither of us had a nice word to say to the other, and by the time the phone call was terminated the damage had been done.

Weeks passed without contact. Weeks that turned into months. Months that turned into years. Not a day went by when I didn't think of my brother and his children. Not a day went by that I didn't regret that awful argument. But I was too proud and too stubborn to be the one to apologise, believing he was just as much in the wrong as I was. I didn't meet Conor until he was three years old and by that time Ethan was six, a fully-grown boy. I was then twenty-eight and in the midst of a chemotherapy battle, unsure how long cancer would grant me with the boys to make up for all that lost time.

* * *

When Graeme and I tied the knot only his parents, my mum and her new husband Oscar were present. We had agreed on a non-religious ceremony, after much dispute. I had wanted a simple celebration, whereas Graeme wanted the traditional white wedding. But I wasn't a woman of faith, so a religious ceremony was completely out of the question for me. Not to mention that a wedding without the bride's family would have been an embarrassment. We compromised on a low-key wedding abroad followed by a big reception at home on our return from Italy.

We invited a hundred guests to our reception at our local golf club – mostly Graeme's family and friends as I wasn't speaking to any of my family except my mother. Unfortunately after the fall out with my brother, my relationship with my granny had also soured.

She had always been exceptionally close to Matthew and naturally sided with him after our argument. We spoke for a while after but our conversations soon become forced. My weekly visits to Bangor turned to fortnightly and then monthly, until my granny and I stopped speaking altogether. Neither one of us really knew why and both of us blamed the other.

I thought about contacting my granny often, but as time went on I lost the courage to pick up the phone. I tried to reconcile by inviting her to the wedding reception but both my granny and my auntie ignored the invitation. After much contemplation I decided not to send my brother and his family an invite at all; unable to deal with the hurt if they rejected me too. What should have been a happy and exciting time for me was unfortunately tainted with sadness. Part of me blamed myself for that sadness and part of me blamed them. I felt a mixture of hurt and resentment; a combination of love and hate.

Graeme and I were married on 29 August 2017. We had chosen the beautiful coastal town of Sorrento as our wedding destination and the ceremony took place on a clifftop facing the stunning Italian Riviera. I was dressed in a fully beaded gown designed by Justin Alexander and the jewels glistened and sparkled under the forty-degree sun. I wore my hair in a curly updo – with a jewelled headpiece picked by my dear friend Gillian, to show off the intricate back design of my dress. My skin glowed with a natural sun-kissed tan and I continued the theme of the natural look – minimal make-up and simple jewellery, not wanting to take any attention away from my dress.

I approached the aisle. My dad's photo smiled up at me from a table filled with stunning yellow roses, my favourite flower. I closed my eyes for a second, feeling the warmth of the sun on my face, and imagined his presence. But it was my mum who gave me away that day – the last person I ever imagined walking me down the aisle. She was dressed all in pink, blending in with the pink rose gardens behind us. I clung to her nervously, terrified I would fall, but I made it up the aisle in one piece.

My mum kissed my cheek and let me go as Graeme turned to me looking as nervous as I was. He smiled sheepishly and whispered, *'You look beautiful.'* I squeezed his hand tightly and didn't let go.

We had written our own vows. Graeme went first with a few short and sweet lines followed by my own lengthy poetry: *'From sunrise to sunset, till death do us part, I promise to love you with all my heart.'* Never once had I considered how quickly those vows could apply to our marriage. We sealed our promise with a kiss, a display of a lifetime commitment to one another. Unbeknown to us, cancer had very different plans.

A guitarist played an acoustic version of our wedding song, Van Morrison's *'These Are The Days'* while we signed our marriage certificate. We had been stuck between Van Morrison and Elvis Presley's *'Can't Help Falling In Love',* but after much debate we went with Graeme's choice of Van Morrison. The guitarist played the song ever so sweetly behind us and I sang along to the lyrics in my head.

A few photos were taken by the cliff edge and in the surrounding gardens, and that was it – the ceremony really was short and sweet. We travelled back into town in an old Fiat 500 – a traditional Italian car, and my heart rate returned to normal as we followed the winding cliff edge back into town. My body began to relax. That was it, the hard part was over. I still clung onto Graeme's hand, though, not quite ready to let it go.

We had asked the photographer to follow us into the town square so he could get some natural shots of us walking through the old cobbled streets. Passers-by clapped and cheered as we walked through the narrow alleyways of Sorrento. *'Bella, Bella,'* they shouted. It was so surreal. Everyone's eyes were on me, and in that moment I really did feel like a princess in my beautiful sparkling gown.

We had chosen a quaint outdoor restaurant for our wedding meal; a garden lit with a soft fairy-like glow that reminded me of a scene from Shakespeare's A Midsummer Night's Dream.

I ordered steak and Graeme ordered pizza. My mum read a short speech and we toasted with champagne followed by a slice of traditional Sorrento lemon sponge. We ended our perfect day with a champagne bellini on the hotel terrace watching the sun go down behind Mount Vesuvius. Incidentally, most of my wedding photos had that mountain situated perfectly in the background. It seemed the mountains had always called out to my soul.

After sunset I changed into a lighter dress and removed my wedding shoes. The six of us chose a table close to the hotel band and relaxed to the music. The last song of the evening began with that all too familiar musical intro. I looked at my husband and smiled as he took my hand and we had our first dance to Elvis Presley's *'Can't Help Falling In Love'.* It had been chosen at random – no one in the audience had requested it, which was our proof that some things really are meant to be. It would seem I got my happily ever after after all.

Chapter 6

# -A Black Dog-

I have two black dogs in my life: one that is depression and one that I named Bear.

Many of you will have heard of the Black Dog Campaign, but for those who haven't, let me fill you in. The campaign is about a metaphoric black dog that follows its master - aka a person suffering with low mood or depression, everywhere they go; holding their owner back and preventing them from living a full and happy life. Eventually the master learns to embrace their black dog, tame it, love it and ultimately teach it to heel.

I had been tormented by my very own black dog ever since the death of my father. That unwanted shadow cornered me in my parents' hateful shop on the night I lost my father, and just never left. No matter how hard I tried to shake him, he remained a constant in my life – untameable, unmanageable and unbearable.

My second black dog came into my life as I finished my degree. Graeme had promised me a puppy for my graduation present and I held him to his promise. I had been looking at Springadors – half Labrador, half springer spaniel, but they seemed a little hard to come by, especially in Northern Ireland. Graeme had hinted that he would source my specific pup while I was in Thailand, so I assumed he would surprise me with one when I got home. But a week before I was due to leave we came across an online advertisement for a black Labrador puppy that needed rehomed urgently.

The address was only a ten-minute drive from our house. Surely there was no harm in looking, right?

When we arrived at the owner's house I instantly felt bad vibes. Their home was severely neglected – rubbish and dog waste covered the front garden. It didn't look like a place humans would want to live never mind a dog. I navigated my way through the maze of waste and knocked on the front door. A young teenage girl answered and told me her mother wasn't home but we could see the puppy anyway. We weren't invited inside, which I was thankful for. I could hear other children inside and wondered who was taking care of them and the puppy. I hoped there was some parental guardian on the premises at least.

The pup was just raring to go, wiggling and squirming in the young girl's arms. She dropped him gently and he bounded straight towards me, jumping up at my legs and nibbling at my hands. I could tell he was going to be a handful already but his energy was infectious. He darted about the driveway with his tongue hanging out of his mouth, panting like someone had just administered him adrenaline. I couldn't help but giggle at the sight of this goofy black furball.

Not only did he have a vibrant personality, but he was a handsome fellow too. His coat was completely black – not a spot of white on him, and he was super shiny like a baby seal. He looked healthy despite his unhealthy surroundings. But what captivated me the most about this black dog were his beautiful black eyes. I looked into those eyes and I was sold.

We drove out of the housing estate half an hour later with our gorgeous puppy curled up in my lap. We sealed the deal with a teenager, which I wasn't sure was even legal, but we had paid the full asking price at least. As we were exiting the estate, a neighbour waved us to pull over. My heart instantly sank; I didn't want to hear what they had to say. Turns out my pup had been mistreated

– I knew it! His owners had left him chained up outside at night with no shelter or light. The neighbours had heard him howling, obviously frightened. He was only ten weeks old, just a baby, and he needed nurtured and cared for, not dumped outside along with the rubbish. I cradled my little fur baby even tighter and made a promise to him that I would keep him safe forever. He would be treated as a king from that day forth, and he has been.

I fell in love with my new black dog instantly. He was part of our family from the minute I had laid eyes on him. Graeme and I joke about the intensity of my love for our dog, who I later named Bear. My whole life revolves around him and I wouldn't have it any other way. I honestly believe we were supposed to buy a dog that day, Bear specifically. Call it coincidence or call it fate but Bear needed rescued and we saved him. When I got sick Bear was the only one that never left my side. His loyalty and love stretched beyond the limits of mankind. A dog's love is unconditional and knows no bounds. Me and my black dog rescued each other in the end.

Unfortunately the uninvited black dog inside my head was becoming more of a problem. I was in such a rush to live my life I had stopped enjoying living it. I was so preoccupied with the future I no longer had time for the present. When I finally finished university, after three years of hard work, dedication and exhaustion, I graduated with a first-class honours degree (the highest grade possible). I should have been immensely proud, yet I felt no pride in receiving it. Before I'd even worn my blues – my nursing uniform, I was already pondering what career I could pursue next; how I could climb the professional ladder quicker; how I could earn more money sooner, despite sacrificing my marriage and relationships with my family to become nurse in the first place.

I had given so much of myself and my time to my career, I had saved very little for anyone else. Although Graeme and I loved each other dearly, our marriage was far from perfect – is there even such a thing as a perfect marriage? The honeymoon stage was long gone, and the fairy-tale romance now a forgotten whisper. We argued a lot – like many couples do, especially in that first year of marriage.

But the arguments increased to the point that we couldn't agree on anything any more. Our main problem being that we were, and still are, total opposites. Even though opposites are meant to attract, attraction isn't necessarily the be-all and end-all of a relationship. It takes far more than lust to sustain a healthy marriage. Moving in together was harder than I ever anticipated – especially out in the sticks where we had purchased our first home.

The house was close to Graeme's family, friends, work and beloved golf course but wasn't close to anything that interested me. I wanted to live halfway between the country and the city where there was plenty going on; in a location that would have been suitable and fair for both of us. But Graeme refused to compromise, which meant I was forced to uproot my life yet again. It took years for me to adjust to country living – the sudden isolation, the loneliness, the boredom that all came with living in the middle of nowhere.

We began our married life in a tiny country village where the only source of conversation came from fellow dog walkers in the small park at the end of our road. There was one corner shop (that reminded me of our cursed shop in Blackpool) and one local pub that was rarely open and barely bigger than my front living room. And that was it. There were no local restaurants, no quirky lively bars, no entertainment and no opportunities to socialise and make friends. Just me and my two black dogs for company.

To make things worse Graeme was rarely home. We had got so used to living our lives apart while I was at university, we rarely spent time together now. Once again, those familiar feelings of loneliness crept back in and my depression with it. Graeme knew

I was unhappy. He knew of my desire for a different life and my dreams of moving to Australia but his heart would always remain firmly in Northern Ireland and I had known that when I married him.

I thought about trying for a baby but I knew a baby wouldn't fix us either. I thought about leaving but we were only just beginning. How could I give up on us already?

Realistically, I don't think it would have mattered if we had emigrated to Oz – I doubt I'd have been happy there either. The problem wasn't where we lived, or that my husband was preoccupied with his hobbies, or that I was dissatisfied with my career. The problem lay with me and my relentless mind. Even though I had all I ever wanted, I still felt a deep emptiness that I just couldn't explain. I still didn't feel I was living the life I was destined for. I was still unsure and indecisive of what my future held. I was still lost.

Despite studying mental health nursing for three years and learning all the necessary tools I needed to break free of my depressive black dog, I still refused to access any of the supports available to me – supports that were proven to be successful, supports I encouraged my patients to engage with. I remained ambivalent towards mood-stabilising medication or antidepressants, though I encouraged my patients to remain compliant with theirs. Psychological interventions and talk therapies terrified me and I wasn't mentally prepared for what they would unearth, so I avoided them like the plague while continuing to advise my patients to talk openly and communicate with me. I found therapeutic activities such as relaxation and developing creative skills pointless but pushed my patients towards occupational therapy. I was a hypocrite hiding behind my blue nurse uniform, unable to follow any of my own advice and refusing to admit to myself that I was just as messed-up as my patients.

Stupidly I pinned solving all my problems on my big trip to Thailand. I believed it would provide me with some much-needed time out; time to recharge my batteries, reboot my marriage, restore my balance and finally find myself at long last. Yes, I was back to Eat Pray Love. Again!

I imagined I would go to Thailand and immerse myself in Thai culture: visit Buddhist temples, have relaxing Thai massages on the beach, eat healthy and exotic food, go on jungle treks with elephants, bathe in cleansing waterfalls, learn yoga and the art of meditation, and in the midst of this tranquillity I would miraculously discover my life purpose and my true self. I didn't know then that my purpose was never going to be found on some epic holiday. My purpose could only be found within.

* * *

Thailand turned out to be everything I imagined it would be, and at the same time everything I hadn't. The country was indeed beautiful – there was no denying that, with photo-shoot beaches, jungle terrain and stunning Buddhist temples. It had the scenery, the wildlife, the culture, the beauty – it had it all. But unfortunately it wasn't the Eat Pray Love experience I had been hoping for. Mainly because I was too busy drinking and running away from myself and my unsolvable problems.

Katie and I spent the first week of our trip exploring temples, feeding and bathing elephants, soaring through jungle tops on zip wires and visiting traditional Thai street markets. We ticked off all the standard bucket-list activities. I even got a traditional Thai bamboo tattoo of an elephant on my ribcage. We were definitely living the dream.

On week two we joined a group of thirty people from different nationalities and walks of life. Led by our tour guide – a ladyboy from Bangkok, who was completely wild – the group itinerary took us from one party scene to the next with a few opportunities for activities along the way, which we were usually too hungover to engage in. The days rolled into one big drunken blur, and despite staying in some of the most beautiful surroundings I had ever laid eyes on, I was too drunk to fully appreciate any of it.

The tour came to an end with the infamous Thai Full Moon Party – an all-night beach party on the evening of the full moon. Katie and I were in our element drinking buckets of vodka and dancing among hundreds of tourists without a care in the world. Dressed in our fluorescent T-shirts and multicoloured face paints, we were having the time of our lives.

But while I was chasing my youth and trying to figure out who the feck I was in Thailand, my husband was home alone looking after our new puppy, paying our bills and missing his wife. I had selfishly given little thought to how my trip, and reckless behaviour, would affect my husband. We barely contacted each other during my month away –something we both blamed on the time difference but really it was because I was enjoying myself a little too much. Graeme would ring when I was getting ready for another big night out. I always told him I'd ring him back when I got home, but I never did. I was usually too drunk and passed out by that point. I knew my behaviour was selfish. I was a married woman approaching my thirties, not some carefree lassie with no responsibilities on a college gap year. I had hoped Thailand would bring us closer together, but all it did was drive us further apart.

Naturally, when I returned home I wasn't greeted with the warm reception I'd hoped for. There was a horrible tension in our marital home – a tension that had been caused by me. Graeme and I accepted we were unhappy and spoke seriously about separating, but we chose to stay together and try and make it work out of love and out of fear – fear of losing the other. It was a tense time in our marriage with one nagging question looming over us: was love really enough any more?

Chapter 7

# -Everest-

My solution to my marital problems were simple: avoid, avoid, avoid. I took on extra shifts at work, preferring to be on the ward than at home. Rarely taking a day off, even though I was exhausted and stressed out of my mind, I found it easier to handle the challenging ward dynamics and sometimes difficult psychiatric patients than face the confrontations between my husband and me. When I wasn't working I was in the gym.

I started with a personal trainer and found a new love for weight training. At first my goals were healthy and achievable ... until I started obsessively counting calories. Then everything revolved around numbers. Between calorie counting and weighing myself every morning, I was like a woman possessed; determined to keep losing weight even though I was already very slim. My training intensified after Graeme and I booked our trip to Everest base camp. Both of us knew the trip would either make us or break us. Our marriage was now in the unpredictable hands of the mountain.

Everest is a goal for many fitness fanatics, keen hikers and people who genuinely enjoy living on the edge – of which Graeme is none, by the way, so I was surprised when he first mentioned the trip to me. I turned it down immediately – trekking for fourteen days through barren lands, winding paths, ice and freezing snow just did not appeal; never mind the altitude and level of fitness required to tolerate such heights. I pleaded, could we not try and resolve our differences on a Caribbean cruise or an exotic trip to Bali? But Graeme was relentless.

Thailand had been my dream and Everest was his. I'd had my fun, and now it was time for him to have his, and I could hardly argue with that.

In an attempt to interest me, Graeme played me a YouTube clip of a couple who had videoed their experience on the mountain. I feigned interest at first but as the video continued I became more intrigued. I couldn't deny that the scenery was breathtakingly beautiful. We watched the pair trek through wide open valleys and dense forest lands, over tiny wooden rope bridges and across glacial rivers, and through Sherpa mountain villages. It looked magnificent and certainly a once in a lifetime experience.

It wasn't the physical aspect of the trek that drew me in – or even the views, it was the spirit of the journey; the chance to visit authentic Nepalese communities: Kathmandu, Lukla, Namche Bazaar, Tengboche, Dingboche and finally base camp, and the opportunity to taste the sensual flavours of Himalayan cuisine. As a foodie I was keen to try traditional Nepalese dal – a soup made of lentils and spices served over boiled grain; tarkari – spicy vegetable curry; delicious momos – steamed dumplings filled with mincemeat; traditional Himalayan teas, such as butter tea, made from butter, ghee and salt; and strong alcohol intended to warm hikers in the freezing temperatures.

I wanted to experience the religious traditions of the Sherpa people, who practice the ancient school of Buddhism; to observe the simplicity of the Tibetan way of life; to watch elite mountaineers who live and breathe the mountains – to even get the chance to speak to such unique individuals, who make a living from guiding tourists through one of the most dangerous terrains on earth, often losing their lives in the process.

It only took one video for me to see that Everest was more than just a mountain and the trek was more than just a difficult hike. The journey to base camp has been referred to by many as the *'steps to heaven'* and after watching that video I agreed with them. I was hooked. I started conducting my own research into the mountain.

I watched the 2015 film Everest. Based on a true story, almost every character died during the expedition. But that didn't put me off. I read Ben Fogle's account of his journey to the summit in his book UP and similar accounts of those who had made it to the top. Fascinated by their experiences, I soon recognised a common occurrence between the mountaineers' memoirs: those who had been brave enough – or perhaps crazy enough, to find themselves in the presence of Everest had changed significantly on the journey.

The fitness fanatics had connected to the mountain on a spiritual level as well as connecting with themselves; becoming aware of what was important in life, what mattered and how valuable life truly is. Such enlightenment often occurs when faced with our own mortality. When we are pushed beyond the limitations of normal daily living we become more in tune with our divine selves. Everest offered such rare liberties. If you were lucky enough to make it down alive, that is.

My training schedule for Everest was relentless. I trained before and after work – whether that was at five thirty in the morning before a long day or straight after night shift with zero hours' sleep. I incorporated a mixture of cardio, strength training and endurance into my fitness regime, which included walking on the step machine with a 30 kg weighted jacket slung over my shoulders and regular hikes up the Mourne Mountains – the only mountains close to our home. I timed myself up and down those mountain hills, ensuring I beat my time on each occasion. Never really seeing how spectacular they were, my eyes glued to my watch instead of my beautiful surroundings. The regime was enslaving, and I took great pleasure in the progress I was making. Every achievement was one step closer to that mighty mountain – and that mighty new me. Or so I believed.

Initially Everest had been my sole goal – the reason behind such demanding gym workouts and the ridiculous diet plan I had set myself, but before I knew it my weight had become my only focus. As I mentioned earlier, I've always been curvy, but all of a sudden I was a slim size eight. My legs were solid – I had quads, actual visible quad muscles! My back was defined, my arms toned, my butt firm and pert. I couldn't help but be impressed with this new hot bod staring back at me in the mirror. But my new self-love was also self-hate.

I couldn't go a single day without training in the gym or without weighing myself. Every time I reached my target weight I lowered the target. The lower my weight the more my confidence soared. For the first time in my life I felt attractive and, dare I say it, sexy. I bought skimpy new outfits that I would previously have avoided; delighting in showing off my brand-new body. I plastered my Instagram with progress pictures of me in my gym gear wearing only a sports bra and thong (against my husband's wishes), delighting in the compliments I received under each picture. But what I didn't share was the anxiety I felt every time I went over my calorie deficit, or the shame when I frequently used laxatives after eating a takeaway, or that I starved myself all week for one night out at the weekend, or that I often woke in the middle of the night to add a forgotten food item to the count. I didn't share the heated rows between my husband and me when he told me I'd gone too far, or that my friends were bored listening to me talk about food and calories, or how I cried if I put on a single pound. No, I kept that part of my weight loss well hidden.

* * *

I was sitting in the passenger seat of my friend Jenna's car with a tin of strawberry cider in one hand and my phone in the other, posing for another ridiculous selfie. My two girlfriends were laughing and joking behind me. We were on a girls' trip – Dublin bound. I was dolled up to the nines, my hair curled, with two buns on top of my head that were meant to look like horns.

My eyes were painted bright pink with layers of glitter, done professionally that morning. My eyelashes were over the top and heavy; my lips overdrawn to stand out.

Jenna sat beside me donned in her Scary Spice outfit – leopard-print clothing and bright green eyeshadow. Karen was dressed as Baby, all in pink with pigtails in her hair, and Barbara, well, Barbara's just Barbara – she doesn't conform to dress codes, and I was Sporty Spice, of course, dressed in a white cropped T-shirt, black shorts and chunky platform trainers. In case you haven't guessed yet, we were on our way to see our favourite nineties girl band – The Spice Girls.

We listened to the girls' album on repeat the whole way down. I'd been listening to it for weeks now to ensure I remembered every lyric. The energy in the car was pumping – every one of us singing even though only one of us could actually sing, and it certainly wasn't me. But I sang along anyway as if I hadn't a care in the world.

Barbara requested a toilet stop for the third time – I swear that girl's bladder must be the size of a pea. We stopped at another Applegreen petrol station and I went in with her this time, even though I didn't need the toilet. I wanted to check my bra. Strange,

I know, but I was wearing a white *'Spice it Up'* T-shirt and was scared it would give away my dirty secret. I closed the toilet door and took a quick peek. Phew, there was only a small blob of blood. I wiped my nipple clean and hoped it would behave itself, just for today. I headed back to the car, mentioning nothing to my friends. Now was not the time. We were meant to be having fun, remember?

I'd first noticed the bleeding two weeks prior to the concert. I'd been at a physio session working on some pain in my right ankle – torn ligaments, the physio thought, probably from overdoing it in the gym training for my big Everest trip, and now the New York Marathon that I had somehow been roped into completing. After seeing the physio I had come home to change and noticed an orangey-red bloodstain in my white sports bra and instantly felt afraid – more than afraid, actually, more like terrified. I knew from the moment I saw that stain it was a sign of something sinister, but I was too afraid to believe what I already knew in my heart, so I convinced myself it was just fake tan, even though I hadn't worn fake tan in months.

The following morning I took a hot shower and decided to have a poke around my left breast, obviously hoping to find nothing and just bin the dirty sports bra – never give it a second thought. Oh, how I wish that had been the case. Instead, I stared down in horror and watched the dark thick blood ooze from my nipple, and I knew. I knew from that moment on. I had cancer.

I contacted the doctor the following morning. My doctors are notoriously difficult to get an appointment with, so I was surprised when the receptionist asked me to come in that afternoon. I was glad to be seen by a female doctor – I didn't fancy a male copping a feel at my breasts. The doctor was young and pleasant enough. I decided I liked her. I have an awful habit of judging whether I like someone or not within moments of meeting them. In most cases my first impressions aren't right but on this occasion they were. I held my breath as the good doctor examined me and waited for the bleeding to start. But none came. Of course, my boob was going to make a liar out of me. Or maybe I had imagined it all, please, God.

Even without the mystical bleeding, the doctor could feel a large, hardened mass of breast tissue down the side of my left breast. It seemed to be deep, near the chest bone, which was probably why I had never felt it. She referred me to the breast clinic and red-flagged my appointment but reassured me it was only a precaution because of my apparent nipple bleeding, which she believed was more than likely caused by an infection. After all, I was only twenty-seven. It was highly unlikely to be the dreaded C-word. I exited the surgery, sat in my car outside and sobbed. I already knew she was wrong.

An urgent referral usually takes two to three weeks. My appointment came ten days later and was scheduled on the day of the Spice World Tour. What were the chances?
I had been a Spice Girls superfan ever since I could remember. As a child I had been guilty of wearing the platform shoes and Union Jack crop tops. My favourite Spice was Ginger back then and I loved dressing up as her. I watched the girls' movie on repeat even if the plot was a little weird and silly. I knew the likelihood of the Spice Girls ever doing another concert was slim. This was my one and only chance to see my childhood idols, so I decided to reschedule the breast appointment. The cancer would still be there in a few days' time regardless, I thought.

So here I was on my way to Dublin singing my heart out to *'Spice Up Your Life'* and ignoring the wet moisture oozing into my bra. I never mentioned the C-word on the two-hour car journey or throughout the concert. I kept my disease to myself, already ashamed of it. Despite my fears I felt like a million dollars that night. I was the slimmest I had ever been – down to a tiny size six now. I showed off my new body that I had murdered myself for, quite literally it would seem, and posed for pictures with my friends.

I drank way too much, smoked way too much and waved my light-up wristband in the air in that illuminated arena, squealing away to my favourite songs like I just didn't care. All the while knowing I had cancer.

I spoke of the bleeding only with Barbara, much later in the evening, when I had drank enough alcohol to reveal my secrets and was seeking her sound advice. Barbara agreed with my GP and was adamant it was only an infection. After all, I was way too young, too fit, too healthy. There was no way it could be the C-word. *'It will all be fine,'* she reassured me, but I knew she was wrong too.

Four days later I was sitting in those horrible blue plastic hospital chairs staring Dr Death in the face, wishing I was back in that arena again, happy and carefree, showing off the body that had completely failed me, singing '*Spice Up Your Life*'.

# Part Two

*we're the mountains*
*we need to climb;*
*we're our own impossible peak.*
*everything that we seek*
*is dissolved by success;*
*only the trackless path*
*is worth travelling on.*

**Ben Okri, Everest**

# Chapter 8

# -Why me?-

*'I'm sorry, it's cancer.'*

I wasn't shocked when I heard the dreaded C-word finally said aloud for the first time. I just stared blankly at the middle-aged doctor with the serious expression on his face and replied, *'That's fine.'*

It was only when the doctor, who I later nicknamed Dr Death, mentioned the word *'mastectomy'* that I finally broke down – alongside my friend. I sobbed not because I had cancer, but because I had to undergo major surgery and lose my breast. I sobbed not because my life was now threatened by a deadly disease, but because of my body. The body that I had just worked my ass off to achieve was now going to be ruined forever.

*'The main thing is it's treatable,'* he said with half a smile. I pondered the word *'treatable'* – what did that even mean? I had no idea what cancer treatment entailed back then. In fact, I shamefully knew very little about the disease other than it kills millions of people and can be incurable.

I was moved to another room, offered more tissues and was greeted by a red-headed nurse who explained that she was now my Breast Care Nurse, or BCN. She attempted to comfort me as best she could, but as a stranger she didn't know me, not yet anyway. She guided me through a rather lengthy pink information book. (Yes, everything to do with breast cancer is pink even though there is nothing pretty and pink about it.) I watched my BCN run through this pink mumbo jumbo. Her mouth was moving but there was no sound coming out.

I stared down at the pink folder instead, in an attempt to make head or tail of what she was saying. But the only word I could see on every page was CANCER.

Eventually I was allowed to leave, with all my information and contact numbers in hand. I was armed with the relevant information to take on cancer. Apparently. I phoned Graeme at work and sobbed down the phone. I can't recall exactly what I said or his initial response, I just knew he was on his way to me. As I left the hospital I was aware of how incredibly tired I suddenly felt. My body felt lifeless; as if it had immediately started shutting down when it heard the C-word, just like my brain had.

My black dog smiled his toothy grin at me, and his big black tail wagged with evil excitement. My overwhelming fear was sending him into a frenzy. It's difficult to put into words, but it's a fear I imagine to be similar to that of a murder victim; the fear they experience before they take their last breaths while staring into the evil eyes of their killer. That's how I felt at that moment – like I was staring death in the face with nowhere to run, nowhere to escape. I didn't know what to do or where to go, so my friend carefully directed me back to her car and, somehow, I ended up on my in-laws' doorstep like a little lost sheep, hoping someone would be home.

I rang the bell and waited. My mother-in-law later confessed that she had been too afraid to answer the door that day. She knew I had been at the clinic and sensed the news wasn't good, so she hid in her back room and willed me to go away. When I didn't go, she had no choice but to answer the door. I hadn't noticed her delay – I was too distracted by my annoyingly chipper black dog beside me.

Again, I can't remember what I said to her when she eventually opened the front door. I just recall her throwing her arms around me and crying hysterically. My father-in-law Andrew had no words.

He just sat speechless and sobbed quietly at the kitchen table. When Graeme arrived I managed to walk over to him on unsteady feet, with my black dog nudging me along. My head was dizzy and my eyes were puffy. I felt Graeme's body trembling as he held me close. I sensed his fear matched my own. *'We will get through this together,'* he whispered, and my black dog stared from one cancer victim to the other, continuing to beat his tail off the ground.

I only told a select few about my diagnosis. I cowardly sent out a generic text message to a handful of my closest friends in the middle of the night, sobbing on my sofa and clinging onto my actual black dog, Bear, while trying to process what the hell had just happened to me. To make things even worse, the day I was diagnosed I still wasn't speaking to any of my family – my mum now included. I wasn't going to contact them now, just because I was dying. I didn't want their pity. Instead, I decided I would face this battle alone. The less people who knew the better.

However, Chloe disagreed and told my brother the following morning. Only minutes after their conversation, my brother picked up the phone and rang me for the first time in three years. *'It's me,'* was all he could muster through his tears. My mum rang shortly after, annoyed that I hadn't called her when I had first discovered the bleeding. Maybe they did care about me after all?

The next morning I was left alone. Graeme had to speak with his managers and explain our devastating situation. I said I'd be fine by myself for an hour or two, but I wasn't. Suddenly I was afraid, afraid to be alone, as if I would just snuff it at any given moment now that I had cancer, so I arranged to meet Jenna. She had received my death message through the night and knew my situation. I chose to meet at my favourite coffee house, Time – how ironic, I thought, as I glanced at the signpost outside: TIME – the very thing I was seemingly running out of.

Jenna asked the questions and I answered them as best as I could, but it felt like we were talking about someone else's cancer, not mine.

I struggled to make eye contact with Jenna, and when I did I started to tear up. Then Jenna mentioned Everest and my composure melted entirely, and I cried into my coffee cup. I knew the trip would be cancelled now. I knew Graeme and I would never make it to the highest mountain in the world. Well, not with each other, anyway. Even if I somehow survived cancer, I doubted I would ever be fit for base camp. I doubted I'd even manage my regular home hikes in the Mourne Mountains never mind Everest. All those hours on that bloody step machine with that damn weighted jacket had been for absolutely nothing.

*'You have your own Everest to climb now, Alex,'* Jenna whispered, gently taking my hands and crying along with me. Except this mountain was even deadlier.

* * *

I experienced my second period of grief in my young life after being diagnosed with cancer – which is unfortunately common for anyone with the disease. It's difficult to avoid the overwhelming sense of loss after hearing the word *'cancer'* – and not just loss of hair or breasts or other limbs and organs, but loss of life.

After the initial shock of my diagnosis wore off, I grieved for the woman I was, and I mourned my old life – a life I had been robbed of and a life I knew I would never get back. Nothing would ever be the same again – I would never be the same again, and I couldn't help but ask why. Why had this happened to me? Why did I have cancer? Why me?

Naturally I started looking for answers and always came to the same conclusion whatever avenue I explored: this is my fault. I began an in-depth analysis of my life beginning with childhood. I retraced my tracks trying to put the clues together. I figured that the loss of my father was probably the initial trigger – that childhood trauma must have seriously impacted my physical and mental well-being, making my body more susceptible to disease.

Losing my dad the way I did also made me believe I would die young – a belief that only added further stress to my already stressful life. Maybe that belief had somehow manifested into reality. Maybe I had believed myself into having cancer.

Then there was the fact that I was a smoker and had been since the age of twelve. I mean, I had willingly poisoned my body with those cancer sticks for the last sixteen years and then had the cheek to ask, why me? Although there isn't a strong link between breast cancer and smoking and it was highly unlikely that smoking had been the root cause, according to my oncologist, of course I blamed my daily ten for giving me cancer.

Or maybe I had cancer because I was a bad person: because of all the drink and recreational drugs I had consumed when I was younger, or the family fall outs, or the arguments with my friends. I mean, good people don't get cancer, do they? As a child I believed God took my dad away because I was a bad child, and now he had given me cancer because I was bad grown-up. Even worse, I had refused to believe in God after he stole my dad from me, so maybe this was my punishment. Maybe I deserved this?

Or maybe I had cancer because I had been living in fight or flight mode for most of my adult life, riddled with anxiety and depression yet never seeking help for either. From working in overdrive for the last five years and never giving my body or mind a break, for putting myself under unnecessary stress during university, for punishing my body by living off caffeine and zero hours of sleep, for choosing to work in the most stressful and challenging environments, for worrying about my marriage constantly and doing everything I could to sabotage it, for falling out with my whole family and becoming even more isolated than before. I mean, is it any wonder I was now dying?

Or maybe I had cancer because I had spent the last year practically starving myself; not giving my body the right nutrition it needed to function and then slaughtering it in the gym every day and expecting it to remain healthy. I'd come home from most workouts and collapse on the sofa in an exhausted mess, sleeping for hours afterwards. Occasionally I had wondered if this was normal but I'd always put it down to overexertion and too many night shifts, not cancer. I hadn't realised there was a disease eating away at my body, or that my obsession with my weight had possibly initiated it.

The truth is, I will never know why I got cancer – but that didn't stop me torturing myself looking for the answer. I now believe it was probably a combination of all of the above that led to my diagnosis, but I'll never be given an evidence-based reason behind why me.

After the why came the guilt, and even worse the regret. I looked at my life and wished I'd lived it differently. I'd wasted so much time being an angry, stubborn, foolish woman and missing out on valuable time with my family; missing out on valuable time with my husband. I wished I had met Graeme earlier and started a family of my own when we had the chance. I doubted we would ever become parents now, or I wouldn't anyway. I looked into my husband's eyes and wondered if he would remarry.

Would he find love again? Would he have a family of his own? Would he replace me? I couldn't blame him if he did. He deserved to be happy. Cancer was my punishment not his.

My thoughts naturally turned dark. Consumed with self-loathing, self-pity and hate, I spent days hiding in the house, sitting on the floor crying hysterically. Sobbing so hard, I literally thought my heart was breaking in two. When I wasn't crying, I was screaming. I would scream at myself, at a God I refused to believe in, at my husband, at my mum, at my brother, at thin air. I was so angry at everyone and everything, and I hated myself for it. I hated how everyone else's life continued while mine stopped dead in its tracks.

I envied Graeme as he left for work every morning; his routine carrying on as normal while I was stuck at home watching mindless daytime TV and wallowing in my own despair. How could he function as normal? How could he go to work at all? How could he leave me here alone?

I resented my friends heading off on their summer vacations and girls' nights out. How dare they continue to live their carefree lives. How dare they have fun without me.

I was jealous of my work colleagues having craic in the staffroom and out at work parties. Did they not know their colleague and supposed friend was dying? Did they not care at all? I started to feel like no one really cared and that hurt and, even worse, made me bitter.

You see, when a person is diagnosed with cancer they immediately enter a club. The only club no one wants to join: The Cancer Club. From the day you hear that dreaded word, you automatically become an outcast. People perceive you differently than before. They approach you differently, look at you differently, speak to you differently, treat you differently; or they don't know how to be around you at all and hide away instead. Only those in The Cancer Club will truly understood how you are feeling. Unless a person has been directly affected by the disease themselves, they can never fully understand your suffering no matter how hard they try. An outsider can never fathom what it truly feels like to live with the assumption that you're dying. Whenever people tried to relate to me, it only made me angrier and more upset because it was a lie. They didn't know how I felt. They didn't know my crippling pain, my fears, my sorrow, my grief. How could they?

Now I'm not saying my illness didn't affect those around me. It undoubtedly did, and I'm sure I wasn't the only one who shed tears over my cancer or lost more than a night's sleep over it. But unlike me my family and friends could still plan for their futures – have babies and raise their children, plan big trips away, take a new job offer, go to work every day, enjoy themselves in general. Their lives hadn't really changed. Yes, I was probably in the back of their minds but I knew that as much as these people loved me, cancer didn't infiltrate their thoughts twenty-four hours a day, every day, like it did mine. They were still able to escape the disease because they weren't the ones living with it, whereas I had nowhere to run and nowhere to escape because my cancer was mine and mine alone to bear.

How could I not sit in bitter contemplation and ask, why me?

* * *

I was diagnosed two weeks before my twenty-eighth birthday – happy birthday to me! I always liked to celebrate my birthday away, so Graeme had booked us a trip to Cannes in the south of France before we knew about the dreaded C. I, naturally, didn't feel like celebrating this one – not now that my life was ruined, but the holiday was already booked and paid for, and I had already decided that this holiday, and birthday, would be my last. Surely I'd be dead before the next one.

Before I could make my final outbound flight, however, I had scans to attend to. Scans that would detect if the cancer had spread, which I was adamant it had. Call me pessimistic but I had already envisioned my body riddled with the vicious disease. It was only a matter of time before it would finish me off for good.

Chloe and Kelly flew over for scan day. I didn't ask them to but they came anyway. I sat with my two oldest friends – one of whom I hadn't spoken to in years, in the hospital waiting area; all three of us trying to make light of my situation, all three of us afraid to show fear in front of the others. After hours of being hoked and poked at with needles, blue dye, giant polo-mint machines that made me feel like I had pissed myself, I was free to go. I walked out of the last scan and lost the feeling in my legs. My false facade collapsed beneath me. The tears started to flow, and my old friends broke down with me.
We stood in our own private bubble of hell in the middle of the busy hospital corridor, no longer capable of ignoring the cancer in the room. All we could do now was wait.

I had been told the date I would get my results: 10th June, the day after my birthday, so I decided to make my last birthday a memorable one and celebrate it while I was still capable of celebrating anything. Graeme and I travelled to Monaco for the day – a millionaire's playground that instantly stole our hearts. We spent hours down at the harbour admiring the fancy ships and yachts. I imagined what a life at sea would feel like – how freeing it would be. Oh, how I wished to be free. A gift I had taken for granted until now. We walked along the Monaco Grand Prix track, which I have to admit was rather impressive – and that's coming from a non- Formula 1 fan. The views were spectacular at every twist and turn. I imagined the adrenaline coursing through the drivers' veins as they sped along the track and how alive they would feel as they raced. I wished I could feel that life in my veins again instead of decay.

We had lunch at the highly recommended Café de Paris where Graeme treated me to a fancy-pants birthday meal and a bottle of fancy French wine. My man doesn't like wine, so I necked the entire bottle myself. Sure, why not? I'd not be having a birthday drink next year. I watched the Ferraris and Lamborghinis pulling up outside the casino we were facing, in awe and slightly jealous of how the other half live. Graeme and I had dressed for the occasion, though, and we almost passed for rich kids. Him in his white shirt and trousers, silver Ray-Bans and shiny shoes, and me in an orange and cream pinstriped dress paired with white heeled sandals and matching handbag. We both looked the part. You would never have known we were members of the working class, let alone that I had cancer.

The casino oozed class from the moment you entered. I sat at the bar sipping on a glass of sparkling champagne whilst Graeme sat at the blackjack table, in his element, thrilled when he won a bob or two. I found myself relaxing in those luxurious surroundings, especially after an entire bottle of wine and a glass of bubbly. When we got back to the hotel I allowed Graeme to touch me for the first time since I'd been diagnosed. I hadn't wanted to look at my body after I had found out it had failed me, so naturally I hadn't wanted Graeme to see or touch it now that it no longer felt like mine. But that night I managed to own my own skin just one last time. When we finished having sex I cried myself to sleep wondering if that was to be our last night of passion together.

The following morning we hired a pair of sunloungers on a private beach away from the crowds. Today was another big day: it was the day I got my results. I wore a bright orange plunging swimsuit that I had bought specifically to show off my small, pert breasts for the last time. Graeme and I fooled about taking pictures of me at the water's edge, posing like a model. He usually hated taking my picture but that day he didn't seem to mind.

As the hours passed our nervousness intensified. At 2 p.m. on the dot I got the call. My hands shook as I answered. This is it, this is where they tell me I'm dying. But the news was quite the opposite. The cancer hadn't spread and was contained entirely to my left breast, or so they believed, but it was very close to my chest wall and I would still require a full mastectomy. I cried tears of joy while Graeme popped the champagne. For the first time since my diagnosis I allowed myself to feel a tiny glimmer of hope. Maybe, just maybe, I could survive this.

## Chapter 9

# -The Red Devil-

I returned home from the French Riviera to my first oncology appointment. My oncologist was the complete opposite to my breast care consultant. He had a happy, friendly demeanour as opposed to Dr Death's composed and serious nature. He was an older man – I would estimate late fifties, early sixties, and was dressed in a shirt and tie. He greeted Graeme and me with a dazzling debonair smile and a firm handshake, which made me feel a little more at ease. This man clearly meant business (although he had extremely dark eyebrows that reminded me of Jim Levenstein's dad from the American Pie movies – Eugene Levy, in real life, which made his appearance slightly comical. He will forever be known as *'Jim's dad',* Graeme and I decided).

Jim's dad explained my cancer in great detail. He was extremely knowledgeable and quite fascinating to listen to – or would have been if he wasn't talking about me. I learnt that my cancer was oestrogen driven, which apparently is the best breast cancer to have. I'm not sure there is any best cancer to have, but, hey, I went along with it. The reason it's better is because there are preventative measures available following treatment for oestrogen-driven cancer; treatments that could reduce my risk of a recurrence. Such measures were in the form of hormone therapy; a therapy that would prevent my ovaries producing oestrogen, hence ridding my body of the fire that had fuelled my cancer in the first place – or something like that. The downside, however, is that oestrogen-positive cancer also tends to be less receptive to chemotherapy, meaning chemo may not work.

Jim's dad didn't hide the magnitude of my problem. He was brutally honest when he explained my scan results and didn't cushion me from the outcomes. I was grateful for his honesty – as well as terrified by it, but I needed to know the truth and respected the man with the big, dark, funny eyebrows for giving it to me. I still respected him even after he asked me to make the hardest decision of my life: *'Do you wish to delay chemotherapy to undergo fertility treatment and preserve your eggs or proceed immediately with active treatment at the risk of becoming infertile?'*

Jim's dad told me he didn't want to influence my decision but made it clear that he advised me to proceed with chemo immediately. I'm not stupid. I had grasped that my cancer was severe. The breast cancer I had was Stage 3 oestrogen-positive invasive ductal carcinoma – a tongue-twister at its finest. My tumour was large (the size of a lime by the time it was removed) and my breast ducts were riddled with the disease. I knew that if I delayed treatment, I risked the tumour growing bigger and spreading into the nearby lymph nodes, meaning my chances of survival would be much less.

Graeme and I weighed up the pros and cons in a matter of minutes and decided that having a baby wasn't worth risking my life. I feared leaving a child without a mother more than I feared never becoming a mother at all. So, on that day and with a heavy heart, I signed the consent form to begin chemotherapy and gave up my dreams of motherhood, which was probably the most selfless act I have ever made.

Chemo is known to cause infertility in women who are premenopausal, like myself. The drugs can affect the functioning of the ovaries and the quality of a woman's eggs, hence making conception much more difficult. I was told that my periods would likely stop – maybe temporarily or maybe permanently, although my oncologist was hopeful they would return because of my young age. Still, it was a gamble I'd have preferred not to take. A gamble most women don't have to take because breast cancer treatment usually involves surgery first, giving women time to harvest their eggs. But

my treatment plan was back to front: I was to have chemo first and surgery later, as advised by my oncology team.
The logic behind this was to try and shrink the tumour before it was removed to lessen the extent of surgery.

Although I had the right to refuse their plan and seek a second opinion, I chose not to. I wasn't the expert here and I trusted my team, but, Sod's Law, it turned out their plan didn't work. Chemo failed and I lost more than just my hair because of it. But even experts cannot predict the outcome of cancer treatment. Every human body is different and complex. Each body will have a different response to chemo drugs. Jim's dad could never have known that my body wouldn't respond.

And as if being forced into making a decision about whether or not I had time to freeze my eggs wasn't enough, that day I was hit with a double whammy. Never mind how life-changing the previous conversation had been, now I had another upsetting scenario to contemplate: there was no possibility of having an implant immediately after my mastectomy. My cancer was just too extensive and they would have to remove everything - my nipple, breast muscle, breast skin and surrounding breast tissue. It left me no room to have an implant fitted underneath. My oncologist talked me through other reconstructive options, but warned me that a reconstruction would never completely replicate my breast. I would also never have feeling in a fake boob and would have to have a fake nipple reconstructed and tattooed on.

In Northern Ireland there are only three types of breast reconstruction available: the first type, as I mentioned above, uses an implant situated underneath the muscle of the breast wall, which my medical team had already ruled out for me. The second type uses a flap of muscle from the latissimus dorsi muscle in your back. The third and most drastic type of reconstructive surgery uses fat and tissue from the lower part of the belly. I, of course, didn't have enough fat in my lower belly after my stupid six-pack goals.

Therefore my only choice was the second one – my lats. But that wasn't a straightforward choice either (when is anything in this game?) because surgery can lead to a weakened back and shoulder muscles, and further complications in later life.
For me that would mean weight training would be difficult, and it would also involve cutting directly through the Arabic tattoo I have on my back – a tattoo I had chosen especially for my father, a special quote I had found when I was eighteen that symbolised my pain after losing the most important person in my life. I looked at my husband and he knew instantly what I was thinking: reconstructive surgery wasn't an option, at least not in the immediate future anyway. At twenty-eight I would be a *'freak'*, and could potentially have to live with only one boob for the rest of my life.

* * *

I was sitting in the dreaded chemo chair watching a nurse flood the red devil poison into my veins – the poison that could take away my fertility, my hair, my nails, my self-esteem, my confidence, my independence and my identity, and still I smiled watching it snake its way into my body. I chatted to the nurse as she pumped six large syringes of chemo into one tiny vein in my wrist. I made jokes with my husband, wanting him to feel at ease. Acting my way through the procedure with an Oscar-winning performance, hiding the terror I felt within.

Six hours later I left the hospital feeling relatively normal. I hadn't mutated into some kind of chemo monster, not yet at least. I came home, got into my new Princess Jasmine jammies that Gillian had bought me and drank the ginger tea my cousin had brought up to help with sickness. So far so good. I sat in my new massage chair that Graeme had purchased to keep Bear from jumping up at me during treatment. Even though I hated the thing from the moment

I saw it, I sat in it to appease him, but to me it was a sick chair. My sick chair.

I was on to my fourth episode of The Walking Dead series and still no sign of any sickness when I found myself surprisingly hungry – actually I was famished. I hadn't eaten a thing all day in fear of bringing it back up again but all seemed well on the sickness Western Front. Stupidly I thought it was a good idea to order Chinese – chicken curry and egg fried rice, my favourite dish. Surely I deserved a treat after what I'd been through that day, and I figured I had been lucky to somehow escape the sickness.

Less than an hour later I seriously regretted that chicken curry. After heaving up the last bloody grain of rice followed by my entire stomach contents, I made a mental note to myself: in future no more takeaways after chemo. I was shocked at how quickly the sickness kicked in. One minute I was sitting comfortably in my sick chair, belly full of Chinese, Bear curled up at my feet, watching zombies on the TV, and the next minute I felt a severe rush of heat coursing through my body and began vomiting uncontrollably. The anti-sickness meds hadn't even scratched the surface.

As the night progressed the sickness got worse, even though there was nothing left in my stomach to bring up. I genuinely believed this was the end – that I'd been obliviated by the first round of chemo. Ding, ding, knocked out in the first round. I moved into the spare room to avoid waking Graeme every ten minutes or so when another wave of sickness washed over me, and eventually gave up on a bed altogether, making the cold bathroom floor my permanent residence for the night.

If you imagine that first dose of chemo as worse than your worst hangover – the type where you can't move from bed for days and lose half a stone in vomit – well, yes, chemo hangover was a whole new level of hell. My head pounded as if my skull was caving in. My body went from boiling to freezing in a matter of seconds. My jammies were drenched in sweat. My pulse raced so hard and fast I could hear it pounding in my ears. My hands shook, my legs shook – everything shook. I felt dizzy and light-headed, and I just couldn't stop being sick. I spent the rest of the night curled round my toilet bowl, sobbing my broken heart out. I contemplated just ending it all – going straight to hell would surely be kinder than enduring eighteen weeks of this!

To make the whole situation even more upsetting, my dear husband slept through the entire thing. So much for *'We will get through this together',* huh! By 6 a.m. I felt so weak I started to worry that my heart would just give out. I crawled to the bedroom and woke Graeme, told him to ring the emergency chemo helpline and made my way back to the bathroom to vomit some more. Graeme was told to bring me to hospital immediately. My feet could barely carry me out of the car and up to the ward (which of course had to be on the top floor at the very back of the corridor). I clung to Graeme with all my might while secretly considering pushing him down the escalator.

The staff had a bed prepared for me already. A young nurse completed my admission as I lay with a cardboard kidney dish on my lap, vomiting between questions and answers. I saw the pity in her face as well as the fear in her eyes; the realisation that her patient was so young, and, holy shit, this could happen to her too. I was living proof that cancer didn't discriminate – it didn't care about age, race or gender. It could appear in anyone and I knew that scared people who met me.

The young nurse gave me anti-sickness injections and started running IV fluids. Eventually the sickness subsided and I finally got some rest. Graeme stayed with me, trying to make up for his sleeping beauty act during the night. I arranged for Georgia – my friend from uni, to take his place for an hour while he fetched me an overnight bag. She tried to keep my spirts up, bringing me new jammies and treats, but all I wanted to do was cry.

I spent the next two days in hospital staring at the empty ceiling and feeling utterly hopeless, trying to understand what the fuck was happening to me. How could my body – that had been so strong only days ago, now be such a fragile mess? Even worse, how was my body going to survive five months of this torture? Just one dose of chemo had completely annihilated me. I lay in my hospital bed wondering if it would be easier to refuse the next dose of chemo and allow cancer to take me sooner rather than later. I mean, it would kill me eventually, so why prolong the inevitable?

* * *

For those of you unfamiliar with the science behind chemotherapy, here's a quick lesson: chemotherapy is injected directly into your veins and then circulates through your body via the bloodstream. The drugs are to target and kill cancer cells.

When a person has cancer, the cell mutates and divides into two cells. Unlike healthy, normal cells, cancerous cells divide much more rapidly. They split into two, then four, then eight, until there's a mass of mutated cells. This mass of cells eventually becomes a lump known as a tumour. Chemo is used to kill off those crafty rapid-firing cancer cells, but unfortunately it can also kill off healthy cells in the process. The healthy, non-cancerous cells in the body that are constantly growing, dividing and continuously renewing themselves – your hair, nails, bone marrow, skin (the largest cell in the human body) and the cells lining your digestive system – are also fair game. Chemo targets cells with rapid growth, which unfortunately means it can also target those healthy cells, hence why people who are receiving chemotherapy often lose their hair and nails, can experience extreme bone pain and often have bowel issues during treatment. So, to wrap it all up: chemo kills the bad cells and the good cells, leaving little alive in the process. In the end, the body will eventually repair itself, but in the meantime I was stuck with one that had been completely ruined.

First there was the hair loss, which began exactly two weeks after my first dose of chemo. My hair was wet, having just washed it, and I was combing it through when it started falling out in large chunks into my lap. I had said from the very beginning that I would take my own hair – I wasn't going to give cancer the opportunity, but that didn't stop me crying for hours upon hours at the concept of having to brave the shave. Losing my hair was heartbreaking. It was never *'only hair',* as people would often say to me, it was my identity, my femininity, a part of me. If it were *'only hair',* why didn't everyone else shave their heads too?

In the end, I lost more than the hair on my head – I lost my eyelashes, my eyebrows and all my body hair, which was ironic considering I had tried to rid myself of said body hair since I was a teen. However I felt no joy when I asked the hairdresser to shave my head, or when my pubes came out in clumps, or when my eyebrows and eyelashes suddenly disappeared from my face. After years of wishing to be hair free I got my damn wish and I was miserable for it.

When people think of chemo they automatically think of the obvious side effects: the vomiting, dramatic weight loss, male and female baldness, but what about the other side effects – the ones that aren't talked about? We know very little about them, me included until I experienced them for myself. I didn't know about the night sweats – or for me night chills, the insane insomnia that drove me to tears, the oral thrush that turned my tongue green. I didn't know that my toenails would turn black and fall off one by one, or that I would gain weight – not lose it, because of the steroids used to control the vomiting. I didn't know about the nasty metallic taste left lingering in my mouth, or the constant pain in my battered body – in my joints, in my muscles, in my bones. I didn't know about the ongoing toilet problems I would have to endure –

either severe constipation or severe diarrhoea. I don't know which was worse: practically tearing myself open on the toilet or the very real possibility of pooing my pants in public. Most of us are uneducated in these delightful side effects of chemotherapy. Even when I glanced over them in the information booklets provided I still wasn't prepared for what was in store. I don't think anyone could be prepared for all that.

Chemo was monotonous as much as it was relentless. Every night I'd wake at 3 a.m. on the dot – not a minute before or a minute after. It was uncanny. I'd wake from my short slumber drenched from head to toe in cold sweat and my entire body trembling. I'd run a scolding hot shower to warm myself up again, and I'd stay there for a half hour, maybe an hour or maybe longer; I wasn't aware of time any more. I'd sit on the shower floor with the scalding water beating off my battered body, hugging my knees to my chest and crying silently to myself. Eventually I'd emerge, wrap myself up in my fluffy dressing gown and head downstairs where I'd curl up on the sofa and cry some more, burying myself in Bear's jet-black fur, contemplate my existence and wonder was it worth fighting for. Those nights were long and torturous. When the rest of the world was silent and the only sound was my despair.

One time I woke at my usual 3 a.m. and headed to the bathroom for my habitual hot shower. I caught a glimpse of myself in the shadows of the mirror and no longer recognised the woman staring back at me. My face was pale and sickly. My head shiny and bald. My eyes black and sunken. My cheeks bloated and puffy. I had aged in a matter of weeks. My entire appearance had completely changed. I was no longer Alex. I was just another girl with cancer.

I came downstairs, made a coffee and chose a depressing movie – just to make myself feel even worse. Tonight's choice, Pearl Harbor. A guaranteed tear-jerker where almost everyone dies. It suited my gloomy mood down to the ground. When the movie ended I sat in silence staring blankly into space, soaked in my own tears – tears over the movie and tears over cancer. I was done, completely and entirely done. Cancer had won. I didn't want to fight any more; I just wanted it all to be over, even if that meant dying. I scrolled through my playlists on my phone looking for sad songs that would make me feel even more suicidal. I came across a Beyoncé song, *'I Was Here.'*

I listened to the lyrics and in that moment everything changed. I realised I no longer wanted to waste what precious time I had left wallowing in self-pity. Instead, I wanted to live each day to the fullest and know that it counted for something, to touch the hearts of those who knew me, to be remembered for my strengths not my weaknesses, to show the world I wasn't ready to leave just yet, to prove to myself *'I was still here.'* I played the song on repeat, over and over for hours upon hours allowing her words to sink into my soul.

In the darkness of my despair, my perspective of my illness began to slowly shift. I was suddenly able to see the small positives in what had been an enormous negative in my life. I began to believe I could use the misfortune of my diagnosis to help others by raising awareness in the younger population. I could share my story and show young women like me that they aren't immune to this disease. I could make a difference to somebody's life even if it was too late to save my own.

I knew it was time for my pity party to end. I would no longer allow my vulnerability and depression to sink me. I wasn't raised to be a quitter; I was born to thrive. I started to wonder if my battle against cancer was truly lost. Could I reflect on my life and know that I had really lived it – had I really made the most of it? As I watched the sun begin to rise with Beyoncé's words ringing in my ears, I felt myself awakening from my cancerous slumber, soaked in my tears and trembling with excitement, knowing *'I was here'* at long last. I was finally alive!

The first thing I decided to do was come clean and stop hiding my cancer – stop hiding my truth of the situation I found myself in and, more importantly, stop feeling ashamed of it. So I wrote a social media post – the quickest way to alert the world of any situation nowadays, and shared it. After seven weeks of desperately trying to keep my cancer a secret I was finally ready to speak my truth: the good, the bad and the ugly truth; the reality of what it means to be diagnosed with cancer before the age of thirty. I wrote my lengthy post and with trembling hands pressed to post.

Eventually I went on to share my entire journey. For me it was a form of expression that allowed me to voice thoughts and emotions that I would otherwise have been incapable of releasing. I removed the mask I had been hiding behind and showed the world my naked vulnerability beneath. I didn't do it for sympathy or for likes or for followers.

I did it for me, and for everyone who felt like they were facing cancer alone. The response was phenomenal – hundreds of people commented and reached out to me. Their words of comfort empowered me and their responses fuelled me to do more, to share more, to help more, and so I came up with a plan of how I wanted to spend the next months of my life during chemotherapy; how I was going to show the world I was here.

I started thinking about productive ways to spend the free time that had been forced upon me. I researched beautiful places in Ireland that I hadn't yet visited – beaches, national parks and mountain regions, and wrote them down. I pondered things I'd enjoyed doing in the past and activities I wanted to get involved in in the future, and I wrote them down too. I considered the little things I could be doing at home instead of watching Come Dine with Me on repeat day in, day out, and I wrote those ideas down as well. I thought about small and simple accomplishments I could achieve during treatment and jotted them down. Before I knew it, I had created my very own bucket list – not the typical bucket list that commonly includes jumping out of planes or visiting every continent in the world. No, this list was different; slightly less exciting, but much more meaningful. This was my chemo bucket list.

The list became my new goal and focus – as well as my distraction, I suppose. I wrote down thirty goals in total, thirty things to complete before the end of chemo, and I shared them with the world. I showed those who were suffering that it was still possible to live while receiving cancer treatment, and I taught those who weren't to appreciate that life is precious and not to be taken for granted. Cancer can come knocking on anyone's door at any given time – I was living proof, but by sharing my new life, my life with cancer, I hoped others would learn to make the most of their own – to appreciate it, to live it, to love it.

I planned to finish the bucket list with a trip to Disneyland Paris at the start of November – what better reason to revisit Disney, hey? In the isolation of my chemo sick chair I created a Disney manifestation.

I imagined how the park would dazzle even brighter, with twinkling Christmas lights and decorations. I visualised snow on the ground, making the park even more magical, and the characters dressed in festive costumes in the Christmas Parade, a whirlwind of festive red and green. On the days I was bedbound and crippled in pain I planned my Disney outfit: a furry oversized coat with matching coloured booties, jeans and a cosy jumper. I scrolled through wigs online, torn between a long, curly pastel-purple wig or a short bobbed icy-blue one. At least I would look like a princess even if I didn't feel like one.

Every time I was hit with nausea and fatigue I pictured having my photo taken with Mickey and Minnie in their Santa suits and how I would smile. Every time I lay in bed unable to move as my muscles and bones burned in agony, I imagined jumping on one of the rides at Disneyland – the icy fresh air cooling my overheated body as I soared through the sky. Every time I felt like giving up on treatment altogether I thought of the stunning firework display at Sleeping Beauty's Castle, imagining the snow on the ground and the warm cup of hot chocolate in my hands. I pictured it that intensely I could almost taste the cocoa. I held onto that Disney dream like my life depended on it, and for a while it did.

## My Chemo Bucket List

1. Live through all six cycles of chemo
2. Walk across Carrick-a-Rede Rope Bridge
3. Stand at the top of the Cliffs of Moher
4. Visit Killarney National Park
5. Climb Mount Errigal
6. Have a zoo day
7. Go for a picnic
8. See the Slieve League Cliffs
9. Go for a bike ride
10. Complete the 7 Peaks Challenge in the Mourne Mountains during chemo
11. Visit Glenveagh National park in Donegal
12. Have afternoon tea at Grand Central Hotel in Belfast
13. Eat breakfast at The National with my friends
14. Get dressed up and have a night out at Babel rooftop bar
15. Ride a horse
16. Stay in a bubble dome
17. Have Sunday dinner at The Barking Dog restaurant
18. Try a new dish from the Nu Delhi Indian
19. Bake chocolate brownies
20. Read my favourite book, Gangster, by Lorenzo Carcaterra (the book my dad was reading when he died)
21. Watch my favourite movie Eat Pray Love
22. Revisit the Guinness Factory in Dublin for a pint of the black stuff
23. Eat Italian cuisine at The Chubby Cherub restaurant
24. Keep the fucking orchid alive (I unfortunately went through four orchid plants during chemo – they all died)
25. Train at the gym at least two times a week to maintain some level of fitness
26. Have a beach day, building sandcastles and eating fish and chips
27. Host a dinner party for all my girlfriends at the end of chemo
28. Dress up as Wednesday Adams for my Halloween party
29. Throw Bear a big birthday party
30. Visit Disneyland Paris for Christmas when chemo is finally finished!

## Chapter 10

# -A Photograph-

For me cancer was as liberating as it was controlling. Before cancer I had felt a great emptiness in my life – as if I'd been wandering around half blind, deaf and numb; searching for something and always finding myself wanting. But cancer taught me to slow down and open my eyes, to finally seeing the world I had been missing out on. To hear, smell, taste and touch, and to live in the present moment rather than the pain of my past or the uncertainty of my future. Cancer taught me to appreciate life in all its glory, and I wanted to remember it all – every precious moment, so I photographed the entire journey and shared the truth of what cancer meant to me.

I had always had a love for photography, even though I'd never studied it. I had a natural flair for capturing the perfect image, so I used this to my advantage to capture life as I knew it. To portray not only what cancer looked like but also what it felt like, and how it changes our perception of the world around us. Nature became my muse and I found myself in awe of this free gift to mankind. A gift I hadn't had the time to acknowledge until now – the detail in a single flower, the grooves in an old oak tree, the simplicity of a ripple on a still, black lake. Images that had never caught my eye before now.

I had been blind to it all – too busy living, except that I wasn't really living. I was merely existing. I had never fully understood that my life was a gift and that was what I captured in my photos. I snapped this one beautiful life I had been gifted with and created an album for moments otherwise lost in time. I shot the entire cancer journey from start to finish, ensuring I had visual evidence of the good times and the bad so I'd never forget the very thing that tried to break me.

The endless tears, the belly laughs, the baldness, the heartache, the sick days, the achievements, the pain, the loss, the uncertainty and all the possibility. I wanted to remember it all. And I was praised for it, surprisingly, for showing the cruelty and the irony of living with a life-threatening illness and all it entails.

People found my photos and accompanying words inspiring – a word I never imagined to describe me. Apparently my social media posts and images were refreshing. Somehow I ended up changing more than just my own life – I changed other people's without ever even meeting them, all with a handful of photos and a few words of wisdom. And in the end this filled with me more pride than any degree or amount of success or travel experience could ever give me.

I must confess, though, that my favourite photos of my cancer journey weren't actually taken by me. They were taken by my friend, and fellow photographer, Gillian during a weekend trip to Letterkenny – a town in County Donegal. I had chosen this town specifically because its location is close to two of my bucket-list challenges: Mount Errigal and the Slieve League Cliffs.

We tackled the mountain on Day 1. Now Errigal is certainly no Everest, but it's still a challenge nonetheless. Interestingly, at the foot of Errigal stands a stone monument built in honor of the famous Irish athlete, Jason Black, after his successful summit of Everest. I took a photo of his words engraved into the stone: *'No mountain is too high or no problem too big to conquer.'* I was one of the few who could truly relate to his words. Cancer was my mountain and a problem I was determined to conquer.

It seemed Everest was still calling my name, or perhaps just mountains in general – I certainly climbed a lot of them during treatment. I had no previous love for hiking other than the physical challenge it provided. I had never really stopped to just breathe in the peace and tranquillity of the mountains before, but now that I was staring death in the face the mountains had become one of the few places I felt free from its vicious grip. Free from fear. Free from my cancerous nightmare. Each climb proved to be an emotional struggle as well as a physical battle – Errigal included. A test of me against me, or me versus cancer, or my mind versus my decaying body. I stared at Errigal's steep incline as if she were Everest herself. And I was determined to conquer her.

I was on to chemo number five and was suffering severe fatigue, breathlessness, joint and bone pain – just to make my challenge even more difficult. Although Errigal is only 751 metres above sea level, and one of the smaller mountains I climbed during chemotherapy, it was by far the toughest and my favourite mountain of them all. I spent quite some time on that mountaintop gazing out at a whole new world before my eyes. I watched the clouds float dreamily by, felt the wind cut across my face, smelt the crispness of the unpolluted air and experienced something changing inside me.

I knew I wasn't the same person I had been prior to this cancer journey. I was different somehow. Oddly enough I felt more myself with cancer than I had ever felt without it, and all this change was captured in a single photograph. A photograph of me standing tall and triumphant on a mountaintop with my bare face on show – not just make-up free but eyebrow and eyelash free too. My skin was as pale as a white A4 sheet of paper, my golden-brown wig was matted from my sweat and tussled and untamed in the wind. My face was puffy from the drugs that were keeping me alive. My hips and thighs had returned to their curvy, plump selves – wide, squidgy and pimpled with cellulite. This was me. This was my body. This was my face. Bare to the world. When I looked at that photo I no longer saw my ugly cancerous reflection or my chubby thighs or my messy wig. I saw a woman I was immensely proud of – with or without cancer.

After Gillian and I descended Errigal we headed out for a well-deserved drink in celebration of our achievement (after a shower, of course).

For once I didn't care what I was wearing – wig included, or that I had no eyelashes, or that I had to squeeze into my jeans and was barely able to do up the button. None of it mattered any more. I was no longer ashamed of my cancer. It was a part of me and a part I had learnt to accept. I let myself go that evening – drank way too much wine, danced till my feet blistered, chatted to random strangers with ease and confidence, laughed with my best friend and had fun. Yes, it's still possible to have fun even with cancer.

By the time we got back to the hotel I was exceptionally drunk and had somehow lost our room key – oops! Gillian took charge, found the porter and asked for a new key while I sat on the floor slumped against the wall giggling to myself at our situation. I then decided I'd had enough of my showstopper wig for the evening and tossed it across the corridor. When the porter returned with the new key he didn't know where to look, and all I could do was laugh. I literally rolled around the hotel corridor laughing hysterically, like some sort of maniac, with my bald head on full show. Even Gillian couldn't stop herself from giggling at me.

The following morning she sent me a photo I barely remembered being taken. I posted it – my first picture that I shared with no hair – along with the caption: *'When you're blocked, bald and don't give a fuck!'* and at the time I meant it.

When I finally put the chemo album together and looked at each photographic memory of my bucket list one photo at a time, I realised, at long last, that I had found where I belonged. The bucket list had given me the opportunity to visit some of the most beautiful places in Ireland – north and south; places I probably would never have chosen to visit had it not been for cancer. The more of Ireland I explored, the more my desire to emigrate dissolved. I came to appreciate the beauty in the country I lived in – even with the rainy weather, and appreciate the friendly, down-to-earth people who inhabited it. Australia was soon a forgotten dream; Northern Ireland was my home. It always has been. It was where my parents met and where I was born. It was where I chose to run to when my previous life became unbearable. It was where I built and established my adult life. Where I found love, decided on my career and met most of my closest friends. Northern Ireland is where I had been happiest – even if it is where I was diagnosed with cancer. It no longer made sense to me to leave my home behind and start again. I now accepted that Australia had been nothing more than a dream; a dream that I'm not sure ever meant anything to me other than it was what everyone else did. At long last I was satisfied that I had found my permanent home, and I had cancer to thank for that.

* * *

You'd be surprised to know how many marriages don't withstand the test of cancer. I was when I first came across an Instagram feed that had posted: *'Hands up how many of you got dumped during cancer treatment?'.* Surely this was a joke? But it turns out it wasn't. I couldn't believe the comments below. Hundreds of relationships had ended because of the pressure the disease forced on a relationship. Apparently it was common for people to walk out on their partners with cancer – some leaving before their spouse had even left the hospital after diagnosis! Although I was disgusted by the thought, it made sense in some ways. People clearly couldn't handle that amount of baggage. Graeme never walked out on me but I still got to witness first-hand how cancer can shake a marriage to its core.

During treatment family dynamics naturally change. Roles can be reversed if those with the disease are incapable of their usual day-to-day lives. Patients often aren't able to work, and running a house can be exceptionally difficult, especially for those with children. In our house Graeme became the sole provider and I was, by default, the housekeeper because I was *'off work.'* It never seemed to register with my husband that I wasn't off by choice – it was forced upon me. Household chores were now strenuous for me: hoovering made me breathless, standing to cook exhausted me and walking Bear was painful. I expected Graeme to help. Unfortunately he didn't.

The deeper into chemo we went the more our emotions heightened. Communication between us broke down and intimacy was a struggle, especially after the hair loss, weight gain and surgeries. I can count on one hand the times Graeme and I had sex after I lost my hair, and I can recall how I cried out of shame and embarrassment after each of those times. Losing my breast only made intimacy more difficult, and then came menopause. Our marriage was doomed from diagnosis. Survival mode took over for me and soon I had no energy to waste on my failing marriage.

Graeme's approach to cancer was to remain strong, to keep going, to maintain some form of normality, to try and keep me positive. But I didn't need someone to be strong for me. I needed someone to break down beside me. I needed someone to feel my pain and sense my fear. I needed Graeme's compassion not his show of strength. Eventually I decided it was easier not to rely on my husband at all. That way I wouldn't be upset if he let me down, again. On more than one occasion I asked Graeme to leave, and at the time I really meant it. I wrote him a painful letter one evening and ended our marriage entirely. But despite my best efforts to push my husband out of my life, believing it would be easier to face cancer alone, he stayed for the long haul, which I am now incredibly thankful for.

Chemo was a testing time for both of us. It rocked our marriage so hard we were sure it would sink us entirely. But on the day I rang that chemo bell, in the proudest moment of my life, it was my husband I wanted by my side. I smashed that bell like my life depended on it as much as my marriage depended on it. Determined to make it heard throughout the Cancer Centre, I rang it for me and I rang it for us. Graeme and I had made it through our first hurdle with our marriage still intact. Just about.

I finished chemo on a Wednesday afternoon and planned my big celebrations for the Friday evening. Initially I wanted to host an Egyptian-themed dinner party for me and my girls in honour of my Arabic roots and in honour of my friends who had become as much a part of my bucket list as I was, ticking off most of the activities alongside me. But by the time the party came round I was completely exhausted from my treatment regime and ended up ordering ten boxes of Domino's Pizza and stocked my fridge full of Prosecco, hoping this would suffice.

The party was my way of thanking my friends for all they had done for me over the last eighteen weeks. They had been my rock through chemotherapy. Nothing was too much to ask of them. They had all sacrificed their time to help and care for me; never once asking for anything in return. I stood in my front living room surrounded by my girls and felt truly blessed to be part of such a special group of friends. I reflected on the days when I had struggled to communicate with people and the difficulty I had faced making friends when I was younger, yet here I was standing in a room filled with people who loved and cared for me with or without cancer.

These women (they know who they are) saw me on my knees at my absolute worst, and they saw me at my best flying high on mountaintops. They were there for me 24/7 no matter the time of day or night. They became so in sync with my pain that they knew exactly when my breakdowns would occur – even if said breakdowns were in the middle of the night. Someone would text at the exact moment I lost my shit, knowing I would need them.

It was uncanny how in tune we had all become. They knew I was having a bad day before I even knew I was having a bad day. It was like they could read my mind. Their friendship, love and loyalty humbled me deeply. I owed these girls so much more than just a party. I owed these girls my life.

I was on cloud nine, an end of chemo high – a buzz better than any drug. I felt as though I had conquered the world and the worst was over (so I thought), that I had totally smashed it.
My girls and I toasted to that. Onwards and upwards now! However the next day my high came crashing down to the surface when I woke with a sore chest. I brushed it off at first, blaming it on the alcohol and cigarettes (yes, I smoked through chemo). I decided to have a chill day and spent the afternoon browsing hotels in Paris, daydreaming of my romantic getaway with my husband to the city of love. I went to bed that evening feeling completely wiped. Maybe I had overdone it this time?

When I woke the next day my chest was so tight and raspy I was struggling to breathe. I rang the Cancer Centre immediately and drove myself to hospital. The doctor listened to my chest and diagnosed a severe chest infection. I was treated with IV antibiotics and a course of tablets to take over the next week. My surgery was only a fortnight away and I prayed my chest would clear by then. But still the nurse warned me that the operation would more than likely be postponed after my chest infection because my body had to be fighting fit for the mastectomy. I left the hospital in tears.

Paris had been planned around my surgery date. If it wasn't going ahead as scheduled, I would have to postpone the trip until after Christmas, when I had healed. Paris had been my obsession for months – the one thing I desperately clung to throughout chemo. The setback knocked me harder than chemo had itself because it meant I couldn't complete my bucket list. I had failed to complete my goal and in turn I had failed myself.

## Chapter 11

# -Let It Go-

The setback was only short-lived however. D-Day was upon me – my surgery date had come. Mum stayed with me the evening before for moral support but I had little to say to her or Graeme. My thoughts were naturally elsewhere. I tried to get some sleep but woke around four. I paced the kitchen for a while, unable to settle. I got dressed and took Bear out for his usual morning walk through the park and along the river. I watched his tail wagging happily in the bushes as he sniffed about him. I stood and wept, wondering if this was our last venture together. Graeme carted him off to the kennels shortly after we got home, and I cried some more as I hugged my baby boy goodbye.

I arrived at the hospital early, ready to face Dr Death who was carrying out my procedure. When I saw him walking up the corridor dressed in his scrubs, my stomach churned. The very sight of him gave me the chills. He gave me a quick nod as he passed, which I returned, nodding back to my own Grim Reaper. I waited in the busy corridor for my name to be called and walked through door number one where Dr Death was waiting.

I listened to my surgeon go through the procedure, once more, and I nodded along – unsure what I was really nodding to. I had to give my verbal consent that I, Alexandria Lindsy Quinn, consented to have a mastectomy of the left breast. My voice shook as I spoke, but what choice did I really have? I could either agree to surgery and possibly live a little longer or decide against surgery and most definitely die.

Neither option was appealing but I will always choose life over certain death – well, at least I think I will.

Just to make doubly sure I had agreed, I signed consent before my surgeon proceeded to mark an X in permanent marker above my diseased breast – in case they accidentally removed the wrong one, he joked. I laughed at his attempt at humour and gave him a grim smile.

Behind door number two was the anaesthetist – an exceptionally tall man, I noted, who babbled on about pain relief and morphine. His words made no sense to me because my anxiety had taken full grip. Nothing was comprehensible any more. I nodded and signed another consent form – for morphine, I think? – and then moved on to door number three.

A surgical gown and TED stockings were waiting behind this door. I fumbled with the stockings, unable to stop my hands shaking, and eventually called for help. The nurse who answered was young – around my age – and, again, I saw the horror on her face: the shit-this-could-happen-to-me look, before she quickly composed herself. A cheerful HCA (healthcare assistant) came next to take my blood. But my veins were that damaged from chemo, she was unsuccessful and a phlebotomist (a master bloodsucker) had to take over. Unfortunately she had to go into the same vein in my hand that had just collapsed, and it swelled up like a golf ball. She apologised as she hoked and poked at my hand, while I held my breath, gritted my teeth and smiled politely back at her not wanting to be rude.

Finally, door number four – the waiting room. Loose Women was playing on a small TV in one corner. Two older ladies sat in their gowns opposite me, and a young man was in the opposite corner. I wondered what he was there for. Nobody said a word. I gave them all a quick smile and then kept my eyes firmly glued to the TV strongly fighting the urge to either vomit or burst into tears. My surgery was scheduled as the last procedure of the day – typical! It was going to be a long afternoon. I knew the two ladies and the gent would both go down before me, so I told Mum to go and get herself lunch and Graeme could go after. But only minutes after she left, a nurse came to take me down to theatre.

From the minute she spoke, I decided I didn't like her. She called out my middle name repeatedly, and when I politely informed her it wasn't my name, she continued to call me by it, much to my annoyance. Her tone was brash and insensitive as she attempted to hurry me down to theatre. I protested that my surgery wasn't until 3 p.m. but she ignored that too. I resorted to pleading that I wanted to see my mum before I went down and begged her to give me five minutes to get my mum back, but she was oblivious to my request and ushered me on down anyway. Graeme walked with me so far before she turned and shouted, *'No family past this point.'* I gave my husband the briefest of hugs, unsure if it would be our last embrace, and followed the Hitlerian nurse into another waiting area where I waited, alone, for over two hours. For what seemed like an eternity. Like time itself stood still. Two hours is a long time to be left alone in a state of panic, and by the time the clock struck three and the medical team drew back my curtain and wheeled me into the torture chamber, I was beside myself.

My heart was racing that hard I thought it was going to rip clean out of my chest when they attached me to monitors and probes, and my eyes darted around the room like a rabbit caught in headlights. Again, I had to verbally consent. As I said the word *'mastectomy'* for the fifth time that day, I started to hyperventilate and completely broke down. All the fear I had been holding deep within rose to the surface with a poisonous vengeance. I couldn't breathe and started sobbing inconsolably, choking on my own tears.

I can't do this. I don't want a mastectomy. Please don't take my breast away. Please don't turn me into a *'freak'* forever, I screamed inside my head. But no one heard my silent plea. Then one kind nurse took my hand, as if she had heard my unspoken words, and whispered, *'You've done brilliant.'*

Her angelic face was the last thing I saw as the exceptionally tall man hurriedly inserted the anaesthetic and knocked me out.

I woke up in recovery, confused and disorientated, and immediately burst into tears. Again. The whole experience had been the most dreadful thing I'd ever endured. I can relive the trauma of my surgery just as vividly as I can relive the day I lost my beloved father. I can recall the entire experience – the beeps of the machines attached to my body; the whiff of my own dry blood and sweat beneath the blankets; the tightness of the blood pressure cuff around my right arm; the uncomfortableness of the drain hanging from my left ribcage; the site of the drain filling with pus and blood, that made my stomach heave; my feeble attempts to avoid looking at the flat area beneath the bandages, the place my breast used to be. I can remember it all. Unlike chemo, surgery is a memory I wish I couldn't recall. There are no proud moments on mountaintops or drunken antics in hotel corridors in those memories. There's only pain and sorrow.

Once my vitals stabilised I was transferred to the ward where Graeme was anxiously waiting. I was attached to oxygen, IV fluids and PCA (patient-controlled analgesia) containing the potent opioid morphine. A button in my hand meant I could self-administer my own pain relief as and when required, so each time I pressed the button a small amount of morphine was delivered via my cannula.

After visiting time was over and Graeme had kissed me goodbye, I relied heavily on that morphine to get through the night. I was crippled with pain. The surgery site was so tight and stiff that I couldn't lie down flat in fear I'd tear the entire wound open. I couldn't get comfortable whatever way I shuffled about the bed, and as the anaesthetic wore off the pain grew sharper and more intense as the night progressed. I kept clicking at the opioids on tap in the hope they'd eventually knock me out and I'd finally get some rest. I didn't worry that I might be using too much morphine – the machine locks out after each dose is administered and won't release any more drugs until safe to do so. I eventually got a few hours of drug-induced rest and that was all that mattered to me.

The following morning my nurse said that I'd most likely be discharged that afternoon. The majority of patients who have breast surgery are only kept in for one night as long as they don't live alone and have family members who can help them. The aftercare following a mastectomy is very similar to that of caesarean: no lifting, no cleaning, no driving, etc., which suited because I had very little movement in my left arm where they had carried out the sentinel node biopsy – the removal of a few lymph nodes situated nearest to the tumour. They were removed during surgery and sent off for testing to see if the cancer had spread into my lymphatic system. I wasn't too worried about this – all my scans had shown my cancer was contained in my left breast only. I was due to see Dr Death in two weeks' time for my results and I was fairly certain they would be all clear.

Removing those few lymph nodes (nine in total) had left me stiff and sore under my arm. It limited my range of movement and made simple tasks such as washing and dressing extremely difficult. Then there was the stiffness in my chest, where I'd been operated on and then glued back together, as well as the drain site adding additional pain to my side. It was no worse than I expected but I did worry how I would manage that amount of pain at home without the morphine handy, so I made good use of it while it was available.

After forcing half a piece of toast into me I decided I wanted a wash. I asked the HCA for a hand over to the bathroom, but my nurse thought it better for me to have a bed bath. Absolutely not! I protested. With some persuasion I convinced her to allow me to walk to the bathroom as long as she and the HCA accompanied me to make sure I didn't fall. When I finally managed to stand I immediately felt dizzy, light-headed and my legs were like jelly. I knew the nurse had been right, but I was too stubborn to admit defeat, so I clung to them both and made it to the bathroom, a little out of puff but still in one piece.

I allowed the young HCA to help wash and dress me. The wound was still well covered, for which I was thankful. Neither she nor I would be getting any sneak peeks of the grisly sight beneath. I shuffled back from the bathroom, amazed how weak I felt from completing such a simple everyday task, and curled back up in the bed with the intention of a long sleep.

I didn't realise that my IV fluids and oxygen needed to run alongside the PCA, and that neither of them was now connected. I carried on pumping at the morphine without giving it a second thought, assuming my nurse would get round to reconnecting me shortly. After all, I wasn't the nurse now; I was the patient and it wasn't my responsibility. I stayed awake long enough to ring Gillian for a quick chat. During the phone call I became aware that my mouth was suddenly very dry, that I was slurring my words as if I was drunk and that I was really sleepy. I don't know if I ended the conversation or drifted off halfway through, but I was disturbed from my morphine slumber by my breast care nurse tapping my shoulder. She'd come up from clinic to check in with me after surgery and go through my aftercare. My face lit up when I saw her – I liked my breast care nurse a lot. She always had a way of cheering me up. I got my usual greeting of *'Hey, girl'* and big smiles as she pulled up a chair. She started to explain what came next for me but I found myself spacing out again. Her lips were moving but I couldn't make out a word she was saying. Everything sounded muffled as though we were both underwater. I gave my head a wobble to snap myself out of my watery trance, but I was just so tired all I could think about was sleep. My eyelids felt as though they were weighted down and I couldn't keep them open any longer. From afar I heard my BCN ask, *'Can I get you anything, Alex?'* I drunkenly asked for some water and mentioned that my tummy was itchy.

My nurse lifted my jammie top and exposed an angry red rash covering my belly. *'Most likely a reaction to the morphine,'* she said. Then she noticed that my fluids weren't running and I didn't have my oxygen in place.

She reconnected me, got me a jug of water and told the ward nurse that I needed an antihistamine for the rash. I gulped down the water and welcomed sleep again. When I woke this time I knew immediately something was wrong. My body felt like it was floating – launching into a drug-induced space. I somehow buzzed for help and the nurse checked my blood pressure, but I was asleep again before she removed the cuff. The next time I woke the same nurse was administering naloxone through my cannula – an opioid antagonist used to reverse opioid overdose.

Suddenly I felt a rush of heat running straight to my heart. My pulse shot through the roof and I was convinced I was having a heart attack. This is it – this is how I'm going to die. Not from cancer, but from a heart attack just like my dad. I started to panic, choking on my own air. They increased my oxygen and reassured me it was a common reaction to naloxone. But I didn't believe them – sure, they had just tried to kill me!

Eventually my heart rate settled and my breathing returned to normal. The PCA machine was removed and my medical records were amended to include an allergy or hypersensitivity to morphine – meaning I would never be offered that pain relief again. I was furious. I knew the machine hadn't been set up right and that I hadn't been monitored properly. And, just to annoy me further, I now had to remain in hospital for an extra night for close observation. I contemplated putting a complaint in but decided against it. I just wanted home as quick as possible with no more drama.

The next morning I was visited by a female doctor who worked alongside Dr Death. She failed to tell me her name or even ask how I was feeling. She waltzed in, closed my curtains, gave me the courtesy of a hello, and went ahead and lifted off my dressing – with no consideration that this was the first time I would see my scar. She muttered that I was healing up nicely – more to herself than to me, while I stared down at the hideous mess where my breast used to be. She covered me back up again and told me I could go home that afternoon.

When the breakfast trolley came round I declined food and just sat letting the tears roll. I was upset after seeing the scar, of course – it was hideous and stretched from underneath my armpit right across to my other breast – but I was more upset at how the doctor had treated me and how dehumanised she made me feel.

To her I was just another body, another girl with cancer, another woman without a breast. In that moment I honestly believed it would have been better to have never woken from surgery.

The next two weeks were difficult but manageable. My brother had flown over the morning I was discharged to see me and my granny. She was unwell and, coincidentally, had been admitted to hospital on the same day I had my surgery. He and Graeme worked around each other to ensure I was never alone, and it was nice to have the help. As always, Gillian was also on standby. It was Gillian, not my husband, who I asked to help me with my first shower. I didn't feel comfortable showing Graeme the scar, not yet at least, so my dear friend had to wash and dress me like a child while trying her best to avoid the eyesore across my chest.

I was still unable to stand up straight and instead hobbled around doubled over in pain. Thankfully, after a few days the pain started to subside, a little at least, and I was able to start my physio exercises, which were crucial to my recovery. My chest and underarm were still very tight – I was sure they would tear as I forcefully yanked my arm into moving again. The exercises were to be done four times a day and I made sure I did them religiously; ignoring the uncomfortable tearing feeling and refusing to let out a single sigh of pain. I was determined I would get my mobility and my independence back before Christmas and I was already dreaming of getting back to the gym and starting my weight training again. Nothing was going to stop me now.

By the end of week two I had managed to regain my full range of movement or thereabouts and I was delighted. I went for my first walk with Bear and embraced the fresh air on my face and the freedom of doing something by myself again. Cancer had taught me to never take such simple acts for granted – even just walking my dog myself, for you never know when that independence will be taken away. It helped that my big black dog had been brilliant since my op. It was almost as if Bear knew he needed to be gentle now. He didn't pull on the lead or jump up at his mummy, not once. Labradors really are the most intelligent beings and Bear is my best friend.

I had successfully showed Graeme the scar and, oddly, he was more accepting of it than me. In fact, he was brilliant about it – emphasising how neat it looked and praising Dr Death's handiwork. Maybe we could learn to live with this after all? I thought. But I remained ambivalent about the scar, refusing to pay it much attention. I was so focused on my physical healing that I wasn't ready to deal with the psychology of it at the same time. I avoided the mirror when possible and kept my eyes firmly glued ahead whenever I was naked or in the shower. Occasionally I would allow myself a sneak peek, just to check for any signs of infection, but other than that I did my best to avoid the surgery site entirely.

I had been given a softie in replacement of my left breast – a little soft cushion that slotted into my post-surgery pocketed bra, but the surgery site was still very raw and sensitive to touch, so I avoided wearing it when I could help it. Instead, I wore baggy jumpers and tried to disguise my one remaining boob underneath. I hated the sight of that one boob possibly more than the scar itself. It just hung there like an ugly freak of nature. I felt it no longer belonged to me. To me, boobs are designed to be a pair. One alone was nearly worse than none at all.

But despite my avoidance of my one breast, I was genuinely happy with my post-surgery progress. I felt that old spark of energy returning – the old Alex was starting to make a comeback. This time bigger and better than ever, I decided. Once I received my biopsy results and got the all clear, I could finally move on with my life.

Both Graeme and I were feeling optimistic when results day came round. I wore make-up for the first time since surgery, accompanied by my beautiful blonde wig. I even forced myself to wear my softie for the occasion. I was sure today was going to be the day – the day I was told I was cancer free. Graeme was adamant too, so much so that, unbeknown to me, he had contacted Jenna and they had arranged a surprise party for me that evening; inviting all my friends and family to celebrate my first day of freedom. But as we took our seats in the breast clinic waiting area, I felt that all too familiar seed of doubt creeping back in – what if this wasn't good news? What if this was only the beginning of more to come?

I searched Dr Death's eyes as I entered the consultation room, looking for a glimmer of hope as he politely shook my hand and motioned for my husband and me to take a seat. I saw his grave face and the darkness in his eyes and I knew. *'I'm sorry,'* I heard for the second time round, and my heart sank. *'Five out of the nine lymph nodes that were removed were cancerous.'* And that was the first time I saw my husband cry. Graeme had been so sure this journey of hell was coming to an end and the prospect of more to come was simply too much for him. His strong facade cracked, and, like me, he finally understood that I might not survive cancer.

Dr Death handed us both tissues as he explained what was to come: he was going to reopen the wound and remove the remaining lymph nodes. I was distraught. I was going to have to go through surgery all over again. All that pain and fear for what? Surely I was going to die now anyway. With the cancer now reaching the lymphatic system, there was a good possibility it had spread outside the primary breast area.
Surely this was the end for me?
He told me my tumour had been 6 cm in length. 6 cm – the size of a lime! My odds weren't looking good. But it's still treatable, my surgeon said. The only thing was, I didn't believe him now.

I feared the worst, that they would test the other nodes and they would all contain the disease too. Then how would they treat it? After all, they couldn't remove my entire lymphatic system! Paris before Christmas was certainly off the cards now – in fact, visiting Paris at all was highly unlikely. I had myself dead and buried before I'd left the hospital.

Graeme and I sat in silence the whole way home. For once Graeme had nothing positive to say and I was glad. I didn't want to hear that power of positivity nonsense any more – it clearly didn't work! And for once Graeme agreed. He contacted Jenna and cancelled the party. There would be no celebrations now. I rang my brother and told him to let Mum and Chloe know; I didn't have the energy to repeat the devastating news. The rest of my friends received a very bleak text message and I ignored their responses. I took to my bed and stayed there until Gillian arrived at my door. She was the only one I allowed in. She cradled me in her arms as I wept, and she wept, and Graeme wept, and we all wept together.

I was scheduled for the auxiliary lymph node clearance in two weeks' time – they really weren't beating about the bush. Surgery would take place on 13 December, only days before Christmas. I was warned that this surgery could be more painful than the last, and there would be no morphine or opioid-based pain relief available this time round. Also, once the wound was reopened I'd be more susceptible to infection and healing could take much longer. What's more, the motion in my arm movements would become more restricted and the limited movement, tightness and possible numbness could be permanent after full node clearance. To top it all off, I would now be at a higher risk of lymphedema – permanent and painful swelling of the arm. Great! I stopped doing the physio exercises after hearing all that. What was the point?

I didn't leave my bed for the next week – I didn't shower, I didn't eat, I didn't speak. I just lay there in my own sweaty smelly despair, completely numb. Even Bear couldn't comfort me now. I morbidly started to plan my funeral. I chose the funeral songs I wanted played, which included Beyoncé's 'I Was Here,' although I didn't feel I had been given the chance to 'be here' in the end. I chose my flowers – my favourite yellow roses. I chose my outfit to be cremated in – my wedding dress with my bridal Minnie Mouse ears, and I wanted everyone else to be wearing mouse ears to commemorate my love of Disney.

I wondered who would show. Would my granny finally make peace with me now that I was gone? Would my friends who had disappeared off the face of the earth have the nerve to show their faces? Would my ex-partners pop along to say their last goodbyes? I was doubtful. I started thinking about who would get what. Although I owned very little, my possessions were still valuable to me. Who would I bestow my porcelain Disney character collection to? Or my favourite painting of my dad and me that I kept on the wall? Or my beautiful wedding rings? Who was worthy of such valued possessions?

Chapter 12

# -A Disney Wish-

It was January 2020 and I was still here.

WOW. I had already outlived my expectations. Go, me! Better still, I was in Paris, the city of love. Against all odds I had made it to the French capital, to the second day of our trip. My Disney dream had come true. A dream I had imagined from my chemo sickbed not all that long ago.

Although it hadn't happened at Christmas as originally intended, and it looked a little different than I had pictured, my Disney wish had still been granted. There was no snow on the ground, but there was ice at least. The Christmas parade had ended unfortunately but it had been replaced with Disney's Frozen, which was arguably equally as magical. Sleeping Beauty's castle still towered before my eyes, twinkling in the winter frost. I was wearing my planned outfit paired with my piercing blue Princess Jasmine Minnie ears proudly sitting on top of my silver-grey wig – a special gift from a special friend – and I was holding that warm cup of hot chocolate, the one with the tiny marshmallows melting on top. My Disney manifestation had become a reality, at long last, and I was more than grateful.

I stood directly in front of the castle, after kindly being granted a disability pass because of my cancer. The pass allowed me to get up close and personal to almost everything at Disneyland, including the castle, meaning no one could block my view that evening. At least there was one perk to having cancer.

I had endured two major surgeries and come out the other side, albeit my body felt old and crippled and I suffered with ongoing pain from the trauma caused by both operations. I was still here, I reminded myself, even with my shoulders unnaturally dropping and rolling forwards and their clicking and crunching when I moved my arms; and with my back in constant agony, even more so this evening due to the freezing temperatures.

Graeme stood behind me, gently rubbing my back trying to relieve the pain a little, as the show commenced; starting with the song *'A Dream Is A Wish Your Heart Makes'* from Disney's Cinderella, which was enough to reduce both Graeme and me to heartfelt sobs. As the castle came to life before our eyes, for what I imagined would be my last time seeing it, I wondered could one more dream come true? Just one more? Scenes from Disney movies flashed across the castle walls as fireworks exploded in the night sky in a shower of colour; all in time with the music booming through the park. I whispered along with the lyrics, hoping that if I could manage to keep on believing, just a little longer, the dreams that I had wished for, would come true. Warm tears trickled down my frozen face as I prayed for one last Disney miracle. A miracle of life.

The second surgery had gone much smoother than the first, thankfully, although the aftermath was far worse, as predicted. But what I didn't anticipate was waking up from surgery with my arm stuck to my side as though glued to my ribcage. My left shoulder had dropped significantly, making me appear lopsided, and left me looking like the Hunchback of Notre Dame's twin sister.

Apparently the level of pain I was experiencing wasn't normal either. The nursing staff queried with the doctors whether my drain was touching a nerve ending and requested it be resited but the medical team refused to send me back to surgery. As a result I ended up in hospital for five days – longer than when I'd had my mastectomy, and what should have been a much simpler procedure was more complex because the medical team couldn't manage my pain. Basically I was left to grin and bear the agony until enough fluid had drained from the wound and it was safe to remove the damn drain – with only paracetamol for pain relief.

I lay in the fetal position for the first few days and only left my bed to use the toilet. I faced the wall with my curtains drawn. I feared my arm would remain a mangled mess forever, and once again believed I'd have been better off never waking from surgery at all. Graeme felt my anguish and tried his best to comfort me. He never missed a visit and did everything he could to lift my spirits, but I was too sore to entertain his efforts. When visiting hours ended I'd ask Graeme to close the curtains behind him; happy to be alone in my misery once more.

There were five other ladies in the bay with me, and from what I could gather none of them were cancer patients. There were all much older than me and much chirpier – and why wouldn't they be? They weren't dying like I was. I chose not to engage in their friendly chitter-chatter between the hospital beds and kept myself to myself. The only contact I had with them was when I shuffled past them to get to the toilet. I knew I was a pitiful sight shuffling along with my mangled shoulder hanging lifelessly beside me, one saggy breast swinging, my fuzzy chemo hair on show, and a bag of blood and pus trailing along behind me, but I had no energy to try and hide my cancer any longer. This is it, ladies. This is what death looks like!

I gave the elderly women a quick nod of acknowledgement and then stared at the floor, making sure I didn't give them the opportunity to respond. On the third day I decided I would attempt to get washed and change into a pair of sweats. I struggled to juggle my drain, washbag and toiletries with my one working arm, and the lady in the bed opposite took pity and asked if she should buzz the nurse to help. I politely declined and subsequently spent over an hour in that damn bathroom attempting to yank my left arm away from my body to no avail, all the while biting my tongue to stifle my screams.

Eventually I managed to wash and change my top half, somehow, and gladly shuffled my way back to my pity corner.

The lady opposite smiled as I drew my curtains. *'You look better, dear,'* she managed to sneak in before I slammed them shut. I fought back the urge to cry and muttered a thank you from my hiding spot. After an hour or so I opened my curtains, shuffled into the bedside chair and allowed myself to join the conversation at long last.

I learnt that the lady opposite was called Maureen, or Mo for short. Over the next three days I got to know her very well – maybe a little too well, as a matter of fact. Mo was a very open and honest soul. An admirable trait, I thought. It wasn't long before I was educated on Mo's life story. She sat by my bedside for hours when I was too sore to climb out, chatting as if she had known me her whole life. She talked and I happily listened, grateful to lose myself in someone else's life for a change.

I empathised with her struggles and sensed that her loneliness was similar to my own, although triggered under very different circumstances. We had each other for company now, well, for the next day or two anyway, and it didn't take me long to decide that I liked this lady Mo. I liked her quite a lot.

During one of our lengthy chats Mo asked if I was a person of faith, and I answered her honestly with a no. I told her I had struggled to accept God into my life since my father had passed. Even though I wanted to believe now more than ever, I remained in denial. I had learnt that Mo was a born-again Christian and hoped my honesty hadn't offended her, but she didn't appear to be upset thankfully.

The truth was, after I had been diagnosed with cancer I had become even more resentful towards God. All he seemed to do was punish me, and I felt his punishments were cruel and unjust. I don't know how many times I heard the words *'I'll pray for you'* after I was diagnosed, and how many times I stopped myself replying *'Don't fucking bother!'* I left that part out of my conversation with Mo, though; out of respect, of course.

I was grateful she didn't try and convert me because I wouldn't have been able to help myself in quickly shutting her down. My mother-in-law had already made that mistake once too often by trying to persuade me to come to church with her, which I repeatedly declined and now didn't even bother trying to hide my annoyance. It would go against my morals to turn to God now, and I couldn't force myself to believe out of fear. As much as I really did want God to spare my life, I couldn't bring myself to pray for it.

Although I refused to believe in God I did, however, believe that good people go to heaven and bad people go to hell. The thought of spending an eternity in hell was terrifying, and I feared I was never getting through those pearly white gates to paradise now, which meant I would never see my darling father again (who is surely in heaven because his soul was pure, unlike mine). But even with all that fear, I still couldn't bring myself to ask God for forgiveness. I'd made my bed with God and I would stubbornly lie in it for an eternity, whatever the cost.

Later that evening our local minister, Steven, poked his head around my curtain. I knew his face from local weddings and funerals I had attended but couldn't fathom why he was at my bedside. But on that evening, when I saw his friendly, familiar face poking through my curtain, I felt an odd comfort in his presence. Steven only stayed a few minutes and never mentioned God to me, not once. I knew my mother-in-law had discussed my loss of faith with him and he had cleverly decided against a great push at religion on our first encounter. I did know, however, that he included me in the church's weekly prayer practice, and I knew he would most likely go home and pray for me that evening. On this evening I welcomed his prayers.

I was due to be discharged on the Sunday, a day of worship. Mo had spent the morning in the quiet room reciting her Sunday prayers.

Before she left she handed me a small package and told me to open it while she was praying. Inside was a beautiful pink leather book that I had seen her carrying around, Inspiring Words for Women by Darlene Sala; a collection of biblical scriptures and quotes.

Mo had written on the front page, Especially for you, Alex, to encourage you and help with your healing. From Maureen. She had left a bookmarker on Page 81, which was titled *'I Will Never Forget You.'* The page opened with:

*'Sometimes God allows a long period of pain and hardship in our lives, and we begin to wonder if He really cares. He must have given up on me, we think. Perhaps among all the billions of people in the world He has to keep track of, He has forgotten me - or worse yet, forsaken me'* I admit I had never felt so abandoned by the Almighty. However, as I read on and finished the final line which read:

*"Greater love has no one than this, that he lay down his life for his friends"* (John 15:13). *'Jesus did just that for you. You can be sure that the One who died for you. Will never forget you or forsake you. Never.'*

My resistance to faith began to lessen and the tears of belief began to fall.

As I said my goodbyes to my dear Mo, I handed her a tiny scrap of paper with my phone number scribbled on top and a single sentence: *'You are never alone. I'm always just a phone call away.'* It was probably the kindest gesture I had ever given, especially in my current antisocial state, but I felt Mo had come into my life for a reason; just as I believed many other beautiful souls have done. I believed Mo had come to my aid, to give me very particular guidance, to restore my faith in God.

During that second stint in hospital my granny was sadly diagnosed with end-stage COPD. As I was discharged from my ward, she was also discharged from hospital, but sadly with an end-of-life care package in place.

I knew it was now or never to make amends and was pleasantly surprised when I was met with a much warmer reception than I'd anticipated. Old age had been terribly cruel to my granny. She was a shadow of her former self, which was heartbreaking to see. I fought back the urge to cry when I first saw her and gave her a gentle hug; she appeared so fragile I was afraid I might break her.

We never mentioned a word of our fall out, or why she hadn't contacted me after I was diagnosed, or why I hadn't contacted her when I knew she was dying. It didn't matter now. I could see the concern on her face and she could see the concern on mine. She wanted to know everything about my treatment and I barely got a word in to ask her about hers. When I hugged her goodbye I was glad I'd decided to see my granny at long last, but riddled with guilt that it had taken me so long.

I visited again on Christmas Eve. In only a matter of days my granny had deteriorated rapidly and was now entirely bed bound and requiring full nursing care. I held a cup of tea to her mouth with shaking hands and she sipped the hot drink through a straw. I glanced at the syringe driver, which had been increased that morning, pumping continuous morphine into her tiny body and I knew she only had a matter of days. But despite the strong sedatives, my granny remained awake and alert, never wanting to miss out on a thing. I showed her funny pictures of Bear and she laughed at the silly costumes I'd dressed him in. As I said goodbye and wished her a merry Christmas that afternoon, I knew it would be her last. I cried with Graeme the whole way home knowing I had waited too long to make it right with my granny, and I was heartbroken because of it. As Graeme and I drove home I said my first prayer – a prayer for my granny.

* * *

I had been determined to make my last Christmas on earth a special one and it started with the purchase of a new Christmas tree. After sixteen years of grieving I finally let go of my black Christmas tree and insisted Graeme and I picked a new one that year, no expense spared. The theme was to be pink and white. I chose a traditional six-foot dark-green tree with snow-drizzled branches, along with new pink and white baubles, lights and decorations. Never in a million years would I have imagined having a pink Christmas tree – but people do crazy things when they're waiting to die.

Hanging ballerinas, crystal Cinderella shoes, glittering unicorns and fluffy pink peacocks and draping a matching rose-gold garland on the fireplace and placing a shiny rose-gold star as the tree topper, I played old Christmas songs of the past and made my own finger buffet, including the cheese-and-ham cocktail sticks that are only ever served at Christmas.

I decorated the tree meticulously; every decoration had its specific place, including all my Disney decorations collected over the years and a Christmas bauble containing an old photo of my dad holding me as a baby, which took centre stage. I finished off my display with my Christmas Minnie Mouse bears – I purchased a new one every year from the Disney store and they each had a different outfit and design with the year sewn onto their shoes. I positioned them in a circle around the base of the tree in place of the traditional tree skirt.

Meanwhile Graeme watched in silence as I transformed our living room into a Christmas wonderland. He gave me the space to complete a ritual of the past. When I finally finished and took a step back to admire my work, my eyes were teary with the beauty of my creation and the sentimental value the tree held for me. I was intent on making my last Christmas on earth as beautiful and spectacular as this tree.

Christmas morning was spent watching my darling nephews open their Christmas presents. My brother and his family were staying with my mum for the holidays, and Graeme and I arrived early to see the boys' excited faces. Mum was in the kitchen making us a fry while the boys and the third child in the room – my beloved Bear, tore into their presents excitedly. It was the first time the entire family had been together in three long years and everyone was delighted to be reunited. After breakfast I cuddled my nephews on my lap, thanking God for bringing them back into my life – even if it was only to be short-lived, and thanking God I was spending my last Christmas with them.

We spent the afternoon with Graeme's family. Our Christmas dinner was as fabulous as ever – always made by my mother-in-law, and there were two additions at the table this year. Laura and her husband William had been blessed with the most beautiful twins following a difficult IVF journey and two painful miscarriages.

Laura had found out she was pregnant just weeks before I was diagnosed with cancer. My initial delight for her was unfortunately ruined by my sense of impending doom. Although I was incredibly happy that her prayers had finally been answered, I found it difficult to share in her baby joy. Laura and I are the same age, yet our lives couldn't have been further apart. Hers was full of joy and mine full of misery. Knowing I was unlikely to ever carry a child of my own only made it more difficult to share in my sister-in-law's happiness – not to mention I believed I'd be dead by the end of the year! I think that's a difficult situation for any friend to handle, even the best of ones.

At a time when Laura and her family were excitedly preparing for the twins' arrival, Graeme and I were locked in a battle for my life, and the dynamics of our relationship soon turned sour. Naturally my in-laws' focus was on Laura and the twins, not me and my cancer. I tried at first to include myself in the baby prep, but visiting Mamas & Papas and attending a baby shower full of mummies or soon-to-be mummies was just too much in the end. It wasn't long before I isolated myself from my in-laws and began to resent their new-found happiness. As awful as it sounds, I admit I was bitter towards them – not because Laura was expecting, but because I felt so incredibly let down by a family I was so attached to. When I needed their support more than ever, I hadn't received it.

When the twins were born I made my excuses not to visit them in hospital, and when the family arrived home a few days later I had to brace myself before I entered. At first I was reluctant to even hold baby Milo or baby Molly, knowing it would upset me too much, and I was more emotional with Molly because I had so desperately wanted a daughter of my own. When I did visit Laura and her beautiful twins I cried every time my sister-in-law left the room, wishing with all my heart that God would spare my life and bless me with a beautiful daughter just as special as Molly; that somehow I would still get the chance to become a mum. That somehow my life would be *'normal'* like everyone else's.

But on what I believed to be my last Christmas night, I finally let go of the bitterness I'd been holding on to. I let go of the hurt that had been caused by two uncontrollable circumstances and I managed to hold Molly long enough to give her a bottle without breaking down in tears. I had my first picture taken with my beautiful niece and nephew – with a genuine smile on my face; no longer needing to put on a brave face. I hugged my sister Laura and shared a toast with my in-laws to another beautiful Christmas, smiling for our standard family photo and knowing my last Christmas had been a perfect one.

## Chapter 13

# -The Church On The Hill-

It was New Year's Eve. The end of 2019 was finally here and I had never been gladder to toast the end of a year goodbye – goodbye 2019 and good riddance. I hoped 2020 would be more forgiving and far less painful, starting with my second surgery results.

The evening before judgement day, the second time around, I allowed Steven the minister to come into our home and say a prayer. Graeme and I closed our eyes while the minister spoke the most beautiful words and I broke down in tears. It was the first time I had allowed God into my home and into my heart since the loss of my father. It was the first time I felt the Lord's presence and it was the first time I really, really needed it.

This time when I searched Dr Death's eyes I saw that tiny flicker of light that is hope. Less than half of the lymph nodes removed had been cancerous, and there was no *'I'm sorry'* this time. At last, it was good news. Dr Death remained adamant that my cancer was still treatable, and I was to begin the next stage of treatment – radiotherapy. I wouldn't see Dr Death for another six months, until my annual mammogram. Well, thank God for that!

But it wasn't looking like 2020 was going to be a forgiving year after all. It had only just begun and it was already tainted with sadness. Only days after my promising results and small victory against cancer, my granny lost her battle with COPD. She passed in the early hours with her son and daughters by her side. I drove down as soon as I heard the news, arriving just before the undertakers, which gave me time to say goodbye to her alone. She was lying in the bed as if she were sleeping but her body was now cold to the touch.

Her eyes were closed and her mouth hung open, and the syringe driver was still pumping morphine into her now lifeless body causing her arm to swell. I removed the needle, kissed her forehead and whispered my final goodbye to my grandmother; fighting back my tears as I said my farewells to the women who had given me a home when I had nowhere else to go; the woman who had given me another chance at happiness; the woman who had changed my life. Despite all the pain we had caused each other, I knew she had loved me, and I had loved her. That was all I could hold on to now.

The week after we buried my granny I was to attend my next oncology appointment, this time at the Cancer Centre in Belfast, and I wasn't expecting good news. My brief period of hope had diminished and my instincts were telling me to prepare for the worst. Graeme was working on the day I was scheduled to see Jim's dad, so I brought my friend Vanessa along with me instead. I had purposely told Graeme the date of the appointment late so that he wouldn't have the chance to get it off work because I didn't want him there. I had decided it was best he sit this one out as I intended to ask the question Graeme refused to hear the answer to: *'What is my prognosis?'* Basically, how long have I left?

A cancer prognosis is usually based on the stage of cancer, grade of cancer, how large the tumour was or is, and if there is lymph node involvement. The data is entered into a statistical analysis that generates an estimated figure, which is the likelihood of you experiencing a cancer reoccurrence. In worst-case scenarios this figure is also used to tally how many years you have left to live.

My prognosis was even worse than I had anticipated: I was given less than a fifty per cent chance of survival. I was numb, shocked and numb. The room fell silent, into a long pause that I assume was to give me time to process the heartbreaking news and break down in floods of tears.

But the tears never came. Apparently I had no tears left for cancer. Vanessa sat in shock beside me. There really was nothing left to say!

The medical team still wanted to go ahead with radiotherapy even though I didn't see the point now. But I was set to receive fifteen sessions of radio anyway. One blast a day to keep the cancer away – for a little bit longer, at least. I was to have treatment every day, Monday to Friday, for a three-week period.

I listened to Jim's dad reeling off the possible side effects I could experience: fatigue - often severe, which could continue for months or years after treatment; nausea; vomiting; skin changes to the targeted area – dry, itchy, broken skin; headaches; stiff joints; muscle swelling of the treated area; loss of libido; vaginal dryness; increased risk of depression and anxiety; increased risk of lymphoedema; increased risk of osteoporosis - thinning and weakening of the bones; and increased risk of developing another type of cancer. How delightful!

After enduring three weeks of radio hell I was then to start hormone therapy to prevent my body producing the female hormone oestrogen – the hormone my cancer was driven by. I would receive a monthly implant into my stomach that would temporarily stop my ovaries functioning and put me in medically-induced menopause. I was prewarned that many young women like myself found the menopausal symptoms intolerable and ended up opting against treatment.

I listened to Jim's dad reeling off the next set of side effects, which included hot flushes; vaginal dryness; decreased libido or other sexual side effects; sleep disturbance; memory changes;

mood changes; low mood or anxiety; weight gain; and urinary incontinence. So, basically, my sex life was out the window at twenty-eight years old.

I was given a few days to consider the recommended treatment but my decision was already made.

On my return from Paris, despite all those horrible possible side effects, I would begin radiotherapy and follow it with hormone treatment. The treatment, I was told, could increase my chance of survival by six per cent – hardly worth bothering, you may say, but I didn't have room to gamble; the odds were certainly against me now. I was locked in a fifty-fifty roulette battle for my life: the red numbers on the table represented a tiny chance of survival; the black was certain death. Of course I chose to stick all my chips on the red numbers whatever the cost!

* * *

My obsession with Paris began long before cancer. The beautiful city had been calling out to me for years, or so it seemed. My Paris dreams had begun on a boat trip along the Amalfi Coast in Italy the day before I got married.

We wanted to do something special on our wedding day eve, and had decided to take a boat trip exploring the stunning southern Italian coast. Graeme's parents joined us for the day and the four of us visited the beautiful towns of Positano and Capri before finishing off with a mesmerising rowboat ride through the blue lagoon – a magical blue sea cave illuminated in a soft blue glow. The glow is created by sunlight entering an underwater cave and then reflecting through the seawater, giving a stunning illusion throughout the cavern. It was breathtaking.

But despite my stunning surroundings I was unusually quiet that day; lost in my own train of thoughts. Wedding jitters were getting the better of me now – such a commitment still scared the life out of me. If I'm honest, I had never imagined myself a married woman and found the whole idea of marriage close to terrifying – which I obviously never shared with Graeme. On my wedding day eve I stood at the edge of the boat thinking to myself that once the ship (more like tiny sailing boat) docked, it would be the last time I stepped onto dry land as a free woman. Dramatic, I know! But in less than twenty-four hours I would sign my life away, and all my aspirations along with it – or so I felt.

I wanted the boat to carry on sailing straight past Sorrento, along the Mediterranean coast and never reach land again.

During my silence Graeme's parents had got talking to an older American couple. They were chatting on one side of the boat, Graeme was tinkering with his drone camera on the other and I sat at the very front quietly contemplating my great escape. Eventually I realised I was being stupid and joined the rest of the party. The American couple knew that tomorrow was the big day and offered us their blessing and well wishes. As we got chatting the American lady, Leisa, asked me if I had ever visited Paris. *'Not since I was a little girl,'* I replied. The couple then told me a story of the most beautiful white church in Montmartre, Paris.

I learnt that Montmartre is well known for its artsy streets and hidden treasures, but the most spectacular treasure of all is this holy white church, Sacré-Coeur, the sacred heart of Jesus. Leisa explained that the church offered the best panoramic views of the city as it was situated high up on a hill and was even more beautiful than Notre Dame herself. I admired her storytelling techniques. The couple had visited the church on their thirtieth wedding anniversary and Leisa's husband had purchased a necklace, in secret, from the sacred church as an anniversary gift for his wife. How romantic.

I was intrigued by their story. I hadn't visited an old church since my dad had passed, and this one definitely sounded worth visiting.

I made a mental note of its name and decided that if I were ever in Paris, I would certainly check it out.

As our boat trip came to an end and I stood staring at the stunning Italian sunset, Leisa approached me, took off her necklace and handed me the pendant. *'A wedding gift and blessing for a long, happy and healthy marriage,'* she whispered.

I stared down at the pendant in my hand. On one side was an image of the Holy Spirit; on the other was an image of a beautiful church perched on top of a hill. Inscribed on the silver pendant were the words *'Sacré-Coeur, the heart of Jesus.'*

I was blown away by this stranger's touching gesture. This necklace obviously held great sentimental value for Leisa, yet she had chosen to give it to me. At first I protested – I couldn't possibly accept such a gift, but she insisted, so I held onto the pendant and promised this stranger I would visit the Sacré-Coeur for myself. I didn't have the heart to tell her I had no faith and refused to believe in God, but still I kept the pendant as a keepsake; not yet knowing what a treasure it truly was.

A few years passed and I hadn't given the pendant much more thought, but my keenness to visit Paris had grown and I asked Graeme to take me there for my thirtieth birthday celebrations. I just felt this strange magnetic pull towards the French capital for some unknown reason. Then one random rainy day during chemotherapy I decided to go into the attic for a snoop around, mainly to give myself something to do. I keep a suitcase filled with old treasures from my childhood up there, and every once in a while I like to go and have a nosy through them. I opened the old dusty suitcase that I had carted over from Blackpool seven years ago and couldn't believe my eyes. There, at the very top of the case, were my dad's old paintings that he had bought in Paris, and the first one was a painting of the Sacré-Coeur.

That painting had hung on our breakfast room wall for years. I had always loved those French-style paintings, so Mum had allowed me to take them with me when I moved, but they had been forgotten in that ancient dusty suitcase in my attic ever since. The Sacré-Coeur had been on display throughout my entire childhood without me ever really noticing it. My intuition, or the universe, or my dad, or God himself, was undoubtably guiding me towards it.

I climbed out of the attic and frantically began the search for the pendant Leisa had given me in Italy. Eventually finding it in my travel purse, I moved it into my everyday purse – now feeling a great need to carry it with me at all times. I knew I couldn't wait till my thirtieth birthday to visit Paris – not any more. Time was of the essence and, like I said, my time was running out.

* * *

That following January Graeme and I were travelling on the hop-on hop-off bus tour in the iconic Parisian village of Montmartre – a village that takes you back in time with its cobbled streets, stunning basilica, artists, bistros and unique charm. I instantly fell in love with this artsy, quaint district in Paris. I had my first glimpse of the towering basilica of Sacré-Coeur from the open-top bus and my skin had tingled with goosebumps. I was nervous – so much emotion was riding on this one experience. I hoped the church would prove my journey worthwhile. I hoped to experience some sort of enlightenment or epiphany as I entered the holy cathedral. I hoped I would finally feel a connection to the Holy Spirit and maybe even the spirit of my father. Once again, I was hoping for a miracle.

From the bottom of the mound that the church rests upon, Graeme and I stood and stared at the conquest above us. The church reaches an impressive eighty-three meters in height and I was understandably daunted by the number of white stone steps winding before me – never mind the further three hundred steps I would have to climb inside to reach the vantage point at the top. I was still very weak and fatigued after chemo and surgery. Cancer had ravished my body and I was worried I wouldn't make it to the top to experience the enchanting views of Paris from above this holy ground. But still I began my ascent.

I climbed the stone steps, stopping occasionally to catch my breath, and finally approached the entrance of a massive bronze door, the entrance to the sanctuary. I held my breath in anticipation as I passed through the grand entrance.

My eyes were immediately drawn to the immense and beautiful mosaic that decorates the ceiling immediately taking my breath away.

After spending an age making my way around the church and lighting a candle for my beloved father, I took my place in the pews in front of the magnificent altar. I bowed my head in prayer but I had no idea how to pray – the concept was completely alien to me. So I began with *'Heavenly Father'* to start my first conversation with God, while Graeme sat in silence beside me saying a quiet prayer of his own. I prayed and the tears just kept pouring as I begged for my life at long last.

Afterwards I made my way up the three hundred narrow winding steps to the top of the basilica. Laying eyes upon Paris in her glory from such a magnificent height had me weeping yet again. I wept out of gratitude for the beautiful view before me and the beautifulness of my life; this one great blessing I had been given, the whole twenty-eight years of it, the good days and the bad. For every waking moment I had been lucky enough to experience, including cancer.

I silently thanked Leisa for giving me her pendant all those years ago and thanked my own intuition for guiding me there that day. As my eyes scanned the city below I couldn't help but ponder how much of my life and how much of myself had changed – just as I had on top of Mount Errigal during chemo.

Again, I felt another shift in my spiritual presence; a feeling of calmness and clarity washed over my battered body and I was finally able to let go of the anger in *'Why me?'* and instead humbly accepted *'Why not me?'.*

Up there on top of Paris I made my peace with myself, made peace with God and made peace with cancer.

# Part 3

*It is not the mountain we conquer but ourselves.*

**Sir Edmund Hillary**

Chapter 14

# -Freedom-

Freedom was in my grasp. The sweet taste of victory was almost upon me as my cancer journey finally drew to a close. I returned from Paris calm and collected and no longer afraid of what was to come. I was ready for radio and it was ready for me. I was on the home stretch now and the finish line was in plain sight. Luckily I had been advised by my fellow cancer survivors that radio was a breeze compared to chemo, which was reassuring. It would be a piece of cake, then.

On day fifteen, and my last blast of treatment, I rang my final bell with my family and friends surrounding me – every one of us teary eyed, signifying that active treatment had officially finished. My radio course was done, and I was free to be on my way. I rang and I wept as my cancer friends clapped and cheered at my long-awaited victory. But there were no mass celebrations planned this time – no dinner parties with my girls or surprise parties with my family. This time I had decided I didn't want a fuss. When I rang the bell this time, I rang it quietly.

My freedom had been exhausting in the end, as I'm sure it is for any human who has been oppressed so cruelly. I had gone to such great lengths to attain it that the sacrifice was difficult to accept. Cancer had been my master for nine long months and I had served it. But now that I was free from such slavery I didn't know how to live without it. I struggled to adjust to my new-found freedom and found myself asking: what happens next?

What happens now that radio has finished and I'm spat out of The Cancer Club back into the cruel world of *'normal'* society? Except I wasn't normal now and didn't belong there.

Not with one weird-looking breast and a wig on top of my head. Not with annual mammograms and MRI scans. Not with the constant worry my evil master would return to enslave me a second time round – this time ensuring I remained in its grasp.

What happens now that my body is forced into a medically-induced menopause that I don't understand and nor does my husband? When the night sweats and hot flushes kick in. When I become irritable and snappy or cry for days on end. When my vagina closes its doors at the age of twenty-eight and physical intimacy with my husband is lost for good. Will my marriage fall apart for the second time round or will it sustain another wicked test?

What happens now when my sick period is over and I'm forced to return to work? To a brand-new hospital that directly faces the Cancer Centre where I had my treatment. How will I cope driving past the heart of my suffering on a daily basis? How will I feel when I return to a new working environment and new staff team who don't understand my torment? How will I feel returning to a clinical setting when the doctors surgery now gives me panic attacks? How will I fit back into my old role as a nurse after being a patient for so long? Will my patient experience make me a better nurse or a worse one?

What happens now when my girlfriends invite me to spa weekends or I book a romantic break with Graeme and I have to wear a mastectomy costume or mastectomy underwear with a fake breast form inside? How will I feel wearing these frumpy swimwear designs that I despise? Surely I would feel like an outcast amongst my bikini-model friends in this unflattering swimwear designed for the over fifties. How will I hide my scar on romantic getaways if my husband attempts to be intimate? How will I feel being naked around him when I still can't look in the mirror at my own naked deformed body? How will he feel when I have to tell him never to touch my remaining nipple or even acknowledge I have a boob at all because it makes me cry?

What happens now that cancer has stolen so much more than just my breast? It has robbed me of my femininity and my womanhood.

* * *

Radiotherapy had been one long, monotonous drag even though it only lasted three weeks in total. Every day was an exact repetition of the one before: I'd arrive at the Cancer Centre early to beat the city traffic. My appointment times were usually early morning or late afternoon, which meant I always hit rush hour either way. Vanessa drove me in and out (I was too drained to drive most days). She'd park her cute little retro Fiat 500 in the multistorey and we'd head over to the coffee shop, fighting at the tills over who was paying. I ordered my usual vanilla latte and she ordered caramel. I liked that coffee shop. It was cosy and warm and decorated nicely. I didn't feel like I was in hospital when I was sitting there. We'd sit for a while enjoying our daily treat. Sometimes the conversation would flow naturally and sometimes we'd sit in complete silence; it depended on my mood that day. I'd watch the clock ticking in front of me and as it approached my allocated time we'd get ready to leave. I didn't want to go, but I had to.

We'd navigate our way along the busy corridors following the signs for radiotherapy and looking out for the familiar black arrows dotted on the floor – my very own yellow brick road to freedom. The end was near. The countdown was on. I handed my appointment card to the receptionists; some of them smiled and struck up a conversation with Vanessa and me, making us feel a little more at ease. Others simply typed in my H&C number and handed the card back to me. My name was now 636 808 6256. Each time I was given a black buzzer and told to take a seat.

I headed for one of the familiar blue plastic armchairs as far away from everyone else as possible. Vanessa followed my lead. I avoided the pitying looks from the elderly folk we walked past. My friend and I sat and listened to the elderly man playing his guitar in the corner.
A sweet old man who gives up his time to entertain those who have been afflicted with this awful disease. Other than that the waiting area was silent.

Our hearts melted as we watched a little girl with no hair smiling from ear-to-ear when she got to ring the big silver bell on the wall. The whole room erupted in claps and cheers as she exited the centre in her toy Ferrari waving goodbye to her friends at the Cancer Centre. I fought back my tears and wondered how life could be so cruel. My eyes were moist for a second time that day when I watched a bald elderly woman shuffle her tired body over to that same bell and give it the quietest of rings. Unlike the little girl she had no family with her, no photos taken, no one to share her joy. She was alone in her battle against cancer. The claps were quieter this time as she exited the hospital, which made me equally sad. Her age doesn't change her suffering.

My buzzer started flashing red and beeping loudly interrupting my angry thoughts. I jumped up quickly, said goodbye to my friend and followed my radiographer, not wanting to draw attention to myself. When I entered the room my radiographers, Amy and Arlene, were usually waiting for me. I liked them – they made me feel less anxious. Amy was young, younger than me, and had a sweet, gentle nature. Arlene was my mum's age and mollycoddled me a little. But I didn't mind; I quite liked her motherly concern. In fact, I needed it.

Sometimes I was greeted by new faces, including men's. I felt uncomfortable at first having to display my lonesome breast to them, but I didn't ask for a swap. It didn't matter when I had no femininity to protect. Sometimes there was a medical student in the room as well, there to learn all about cancer for the day. They asked if I minded them observing. I did mind – I wasn't a project to be observed, but I said no anyway. It didn't matter when I had no pride to protect. I wasn't a person any more. I was just patient number 636 808 6256.

I undressed my top half and removed my wig. (My choice – I could keep it on if I wished.) I climbed onto the machine and the radiographers moved my arms into stirrups above my head. I ignored the pain in my scar as the surgery site stretched. I avoided eye contact with the staff as they drew little red and black dots over my naked chest – the spot where my breast used to be. I was measured up with a ruler like a slab of meat and moved into position in line with the green laser beams directly above my head.

The staff gently moved my body this way and that, apologising for their cold hands. I felt myself tearing up as I was forced to stare at my ugly scar in the reflection of the machine, an image I had long been avoiding, but I refused to cry in front of those strangers. So I switched off – detached myself from the situation as if I was no longer there. My mind remained my own but my body was someone else's. I found a tiny black dot on the all-white ceiling and redirected my gaze. I would not cry – not that day!

I followed the radiographers' instructions and took a deep breath in and held it so that the laser therapy didn't blast and damage my heart. I heard the machine fire up and watched the orange light turn on. The sign on the door now read: *'Do not enter. Radiation in progress.'* I felt nothing while I stared at the tiny black dot on the ceiling – no burning pain or fire irrupting in my flesh. I felt nothing at all. My heart was now numb and had no feeling. I was empty. I continued to hold my breath for what seemed like eternity, so much so that my head was pounding with the pressure of it. *'And release,'* Arlene instructed over the speaker. I let out a deep sigh as the staff exited the radio-free zone to reposition the machine and me ready for blast number two.

Twenty minutes or so had passed before I gladly heard that familiar voice, *'Ok, Alex, that's you all done now.'* I slid off the machine, redressed myself, placed my wig carefully back into position and forced brief small talk with my healthcare professionals. I did it for their benefit not mine. I didn't want them to feel uncomfortable around me.

*'See you tomorrow,'* I would say with a false smile. I'd find Vanessa in the waiting area and we'd exit the building together. She was the only person who knew not to ask me how it was.

In the car I'd sit and quietly wonder to myself why my dear friend had volunteered herself for that God-awful task. My misery can often be infectious, I know that, but still she dropped me to my door with her usual friendly smile and arranged my pick-up time for the next day. I didn't know who I felt sorrier for, her or me, as I waved goodbye and closed my front door.

I'd collapse on my sofa feeling an overwhelming exhaustion, physically and mentally. Bear cuddled into me. He knew I was sad and tried to comfort me. We'd lie there entwined in my despair until Graeme returned home and I'd have to readjust my mask, not wanting my husband to see me at rock bottom all over again. When my family and friends would phone later that day they'd always ask me the same questions: *'Well, how do you feel?'* and I'd answer, *'Just tired,'* ignoring the persistent headache and the nauseous feeling in my stomach. *'Does it hurt?'* they'd say, and I'd stare down at my red, raw, itchy, burnt skin. *'No,'* I'd reply.

* * *

In the end, radio broke me. It robbed me of my remaining shreds of humanity and the strength I had left. It made me a broken woman. For months I continued my daily business feeling completely detached from myself and my life. I hit an all-time low after active treatment ended, which I learnt was a common experience for many cancer survivors. After the daily grind of a life with cancer comes to a halt and the hospital appointments, scans and treatment finish, survivors are often left with another sense of loss and a new uncertainty of how to proceed with life after cancer.

It's not just a case of picking up where you left off, which many people unaffected with cancer believe. My life had been cancer for the best part of a year now and I no longer knew how to live without it. I was left with no routine, no medical reassurance and no structure to my life. Although my support network was still strong, I didn't require the same attention now that treatment had finished. I found myself not wanting to ask for help any more and not wanting to speak about cancer with my friends and family. To everyone else, that chapter of my life was over and I didn't want to bore them with my cancer journey any longer. But the truth was it wasn't over for me – nor will it ever be. While I recognised that every day after treatment was a blessing, I also saw it as a curse. What I had to do now was learn how to balance the two.

## Chapter 15

# -The New Me-

I had dabbled in my journey to self-discovery throughout the course of my cancer. When my old hobbies and passions died off, either by choice because they no longer interested me or by force because I simply wasn't able for them any more, the first thing I decided to adopt was the healthy body—healthy mind concept in the hope that it would keep a cancer recurrence at bay. I did my research and explored many different natural health practices, especially to do with diet. There is an abundance of research studies available online that examine diet and its links to cancer, so I figured that nutrition was a good starting point.

Firstly, I decided to go vegan after watching a pile of Netflix documentaries discussing how meat supposedly gives you cancer, especially red meat. I spent a fortune on vegan sausage rolls, vegan meatballs (that gave me the poops), vegan cheeses that tasted like rubber and bottles of oat milk for my coffee that made me heave. I lasted three weeks. I was in hospital after my first surgery when I caved. I had miserably picked my way through two scoops of powdered mash and a spoonful of carrots and peas before deciding I wanted to be a meat eater again. I ordered Graeme to bring me up a foot-long Italian BMT from Subway. It includes a delicious selection of ham, salami, pepperoni, proper cheese and all the trimmings. The first bite of that sandwich was the end of my veganism.

After veganism proved a little too dramatic to maintain I tried the supposedly easier veggie option. At least I could still eat real cheese and full-fat vanilla lattes. I did better with this one. I filled my freezer with meat-free alternatives and managed to make some tasty meat-free dinners that I found rather impressive.

I was even bold enough to order a veggie McDonald's wrap – a cardboard version of their chicken goujon wrap – and that was the end of going veggie!

Ok, so I failed both veganism and vegetarianism. The next best thing was the popular alkaline diet – a diet based on the theory that eating certain foods can change the body's acidic levels. Some studies have shown that acidic environments help cancer cells grow, so a diet high in alkaline foods and low in acidic foods should raise the body's pH levels, making the body more alkaline, and prevent or even cure cancer. But this is a theory tested in a Petri dish; never on a complex cancerous tumour inside the body itself, and these studies are arguably biased. Anyway, the sugar-free concept proved too depressing for my sweet tooth and the alkaline diet soon fell by the wayside as well.

Next I experimented with herbal remedies in the form of multivitamins and powdered wheatgrass that some Irishman from Donegal had drank religiously and claimed cured his cancer. I started taking turmeric capsules daily – basically curry powder in a pill. The anti-inflammatory and antioxidant effects of the herb apparently inhibit cancer induced by the cell cycle. Furthermore, curcumin in turmeric apparently plays an important role in treating several types of cancer, including breast cancer, by promoting cancer cell death, minimising inflammation and slowing tumour growth. Have I lost you yet?

Eventually I had enough of messing about with my diet. My passion after cancer was clearly not to be a diehard vegan and animal rights activist, so who could I be instead? Maybe I could be a pothead like my ex-boyfriends? I'd come across plenty of studies claiming that cannabis in the form of CBD oil was successful in reducing the size of cancer tumours and keeping the disease at bay.

Plus, weed would make me a calmer and collected person, right? I'd heard a lot about the Rick Simpson Cannabis oil (RSO) and decided to give that a try.

I ordered a syringe of the thick black gloopy medicine off a website that had been recommended by a friend of a friend of a friend. It arrived from the Netherlands wrapped in tinfoil to allow it to cleverly go undetected through customs. I was a proper druggy now, it would seem. The website advised that the oil is extremely potent and only a tiny droplet is necessary to begin with – a small drop a day to keep the cancer at bay! I opened the package, squeezed what I thought was a miniscule drop of the black stuff onto my tongue and continued with my day.

Gillian arrived around an hour later to help me with a few things around the house. I told her I had taken the CBD oil so she was prepared if things got a little weird, which they did of course! We had nipped out to get some groceries when the effects began to kick in. I stood at the self-service checkout in Asda and forgot how to use the very straightforward scan-and-go machines. My mind just went blank all of a sudden. My brain was telling me one thing but my body wasn't capable of carrying out the action. When I returned home I could barely string a sentence together. Whenever Gillian tried to talk to me my responses were delayed. I felt like I was on an episode of Who Wants to Be a Millionaire and needed A, B, C or D options to answer any question. Everything slowed down, including my speech and the ability to think rationally. My body felt like it was floating. I kept lifting my hands in front of my face to see if they were still attached; my limbs felt so light and free.

I watched Gillian pottering around my kitchen making us dinner, all in slow motion. She looked like a cartoon in slow-mo. It was comical. In fact, it was hilarious. I began to laugh. I laughed that much I had to go for a lie down on the sofa. I'm not sure how long I lay there, or if I was awake or asleep or floating somewhere in between, but eventually a chicken dinner was placed in front of me. The only thing was, I'd forgotten how to eat it.

My friend had to cut the food up for me, like a child, because I didn't know how to use a knife and fork. The drug was rocket fuel – so potent, and the effects lasted for hours. When they finally did wear off a little I got myself in a panic, paranoid that the syringe hadn't contained CBD oil at all and I had in fact poisoned myself with some wacky drug off the internet. My heart was racing and I thought I was going to have a heart attack – again. I imagined the headlines *'Young girl overdoses on fake CBD oil trying to cure her cancer.'* Of course it was just drug-induced paranoia and once it wore off completely I was fine.

Needless to say, I didn't try the black stuff again out of fear I'd lose my mind entirely. Clearly, I had a very low tolerance to drugs of any kind, but I was still keen to keep going with CBD. After researching its benefits in detail I decided to build my tolerance another way – by eating weed-infused cookies made by a cancer friend from The Cancer Club. The cookies tasted like what I imagine soil and cow poop taste like when mixed together – you would need to be dedicated to the cause to swallow those bad boys.

I ate my first cookie with a cup of coffee sometime after my second surgery and headed out with Bear along our usual river walk, expecting to be home before any unpleasant side effects kicked in. I had Bear in a new harness that Graeme had just bought him – my first time using it. When I got back from the walk I stupidly couldn't figure out how to take the harness off. The effects of the cookie had clearly started to kick in. After a while Bear got frustrated with me and had started to think it was a game, bouncing up at me to play. In fear he'd rip my wound somehow, I decided to go and ask my neighbours for help.

Our neighbours were a young married couple of similar age to Graeme and me, and we had always got on well. When the wife opened the door to me, though, I had forgotten her husband's name and just stood there like a creepy weirdo saying nothing, trying to think of how to ask for her husband's help without using his name.

Eventually I broke the silence by blurting out, *'Is the hubby home and can I borrow him a minute.'* How awkward!

Her husband, who I later remembered was called Kyle, arrived at my front door minutes later and unclipped Bear's harness after noticing a locking mechanism on it. He then asked how my treatment was going, but the full effects of the cookie had kicked in and my mouth was as dry as the Sahara making it impossible for me to get my words out properly. I just grinned my psychotic smile while trying to prop myself upright against the banister, praying good ole Kyle would leave soon. He eventually got the hint and I gladly closed the door behind him, diving straight into my fridge. Everyone knows that weed gives you the munchies but that day I just so happened to be following one of the ridiculous diets I was talking about meaning the only snacks I had in the house were fruit and nuts, so I spent the entire afternoon eating two boxes of grapes and a few packets of nuts while laughing my head off at the commentary on Come Dine with Me. My neighbours and I have never mentioned the harness incident to this day. I don't know if they knew I was stoned or just presumed I'd gone mad with my cancer situation. I suppose, in all honesty, it was a bit of both.

Weed-infused treats became my form of therapy. I found the effects calming and amusing at the same time – and let's face it I needed a little fun in my life. I would take my magic cookies, gummy bears and caramel chews and become lost in a fantasy world where cancer and pain no longer existed. I even brought my magic bears with me on a road trip to Donegal where I and my adventure buddy spent a few nights in the arsehole of nowhere on a random last-minute getaway. Once we realised we really were in the wilderness, we took a gummy bear each with a few drinks to spice things up a little. Unfortunately the home-made bears don't come with any warning labels, and the alcohol elevated their relatively mild and calming side effects turning my friend and me into two full-blown crackpots.

We went for dinner in the hotel restaurant (there was literally nowhere else to go) and laughed our heads off at each other's failed attempts to compose ourselves. The laughter was uncontrollable – once we started we couldn't stop. My friend forgot how to eat, just like I had with the RSO oil, and held a burger in her hands for what seemed like hours while I sat opposite laughing like a maniac. When the waitress came over to take our dessert order my friend couldn't speak, so it was down to me to order two chocolate brownies. But, again, I burst into random fits of laughter and had to ask the waitress to give me a minute. She was clearly unimpressed with my rude and strange behaviour but I couldn't control it. At the end of the meal we managed to walk to the bar to pay. The food had been included with our stay but the wine wasn't. I knew neither one of us was capable of typing in our card numbers correctly, so I asked the barman to charge the bill to our room before I burst into lunatic fits of laughter – again. I didn't know what else to say other than *'I'm sorry, I have a laughing disorder,'* while my friend just stood and stared straight through the barman and the waiter. The poor waiter gave me a thumbs up and said the bill was charged to the room, all the while looking at me with extreme concern. I'm laughing while I write this, by the way – just without the weed this time!

My friend and I hurried up the stairs to hide for the rest of the evening and by 9 p.m. both of us were comatose. We spent the rest of our trip keeping away from the hotel staff, making sure we were out at the crack of dawn and not back till late evening; scurrying in and out of the hotel like two fugitives. Obviously I gave the bears a miss after that, but they were good while they lasted.

Ok, I had had enough of being a pothead, so maybe I could learn to be more spiritual in a less poisonous and more legal way. Maybe I could be like my yoga instructor friend Katrina? She is always calm and collected. I had started going to her yoga classes during chemo but found that the quietness sent me into a panic – there was too much thinking time in my namaste unfortunately. But now that I was past chemo I'd surely be able to find comfort in the silence, so I decided to give meditation a go. I bought a beautiful Buddha backflow burner and some white sage; known for its cleansing properties as well as promoting relaxation and stress relief. To create the perfect mood for my new spiritual practice I started lighting the Buddha at dawn – because I was awake during the early hours and it was a fitting time to train my mind while the rest of the world slept and my street was silent.

I tried to practice mindfulness: to focus my eyes on the flame burning in front of me, the smell of the white sage cone filling my nostrils, the steady rhythm of my heartbeat, the deep breath in through my nose and out through my mouth, but before the sage cone had burned halfway my mind had already started to wander, thinking about what I wanted for breakfast that morning or where I would take Bear for our daily walk that day or if I wanted to watch The Lion King or Aladdin that afternoon. No matter how hard I tried I just couldn't train my mind to shut up!

When I found meditation at home unsuccessful I signed up for a local meditation class instead. The class was held in the evening in a local natural-healing shop after opening hours. I envisioned a cosy back room with nice calming music and fluffy cushions to sit on – something along those lines, but there was no back room or fluffy pillows. The class took place on the shop floor. A hipster woman with super-long red dreadlocks greeted me at the front door, told me to remove my shoes and socks and guided me towards a mat. At 6 p.m. the shop shutters went down and the class began. I was told to close my eyes and repeatedly chant *'uuummmmmm'.* I tried my best to keep from laughing and stop myself peeking at the rest of the group who were really going for it – fair play to them, they were clearly more mature than I was.

The meditation guru guided us through a visualisation technique. We were told to imagine a golden light shining down from the sky into the tops of our heads, pouring through our bodies and circling each vertebra in our spine ten times (intended to heal any back problems we may have been suffering). Good, this was exactly what I needed. We got to the fourth vertebra before my head started to wonder, thinking back to biology lessons in uni and trying to remember how many vertebrae there were. Ah ha, thirty-three in total. Damn it, we were going to be there all night.

At the end of the class the guru went round the room asking each of us what we had felt and experienced during the meditation. The only answer I could come up with was that I felt cold, and this wasn't because of some great spiritual awakening. The shop was freezing. It was the middle of winter and the underfloor heating was broken. I couldn't have enjoyed the experience even if I wanted to. I had spent the entire hour dreaming of the nice hot bath I was going to have when I returned home.

But still I was determined not to give up on the spiritual element of healing, especially after reading Bernie Siegel's book *Love, Medicine and Miracles*, another gift I had kindly received during cancer. In this complex yet interesting read, Bernie discusses Eastern practices of training our minds to heal physical illness – relaxation, hypnosis, meditation and visualisation. I was fascinated with his findings, particularly after reading about his encounter with a young boy with a brain tumour. The boy practised visualising rocket ships flying around his head shooting at his tumour, like in a video game. After a few months the boy told his father he had taken a rocket trip through his head and could no longer find his cancer. His parents paid for a CAT scan that miraculously showed his cancer was gone! Of course, there is no evidence that the boy's made-up rocket ship cured his cancer, but whatever happened the cancer was no longer there and that's all that matters. If only I still had a child's imagination and could visualise my own rocket ships!

* * *

Eventually I came to realise that I didn't need to create a new identity; I just needed to accept the one I already had – with some adjustments of course. I spent my first year of cancer getting to know myself, investing in myself and feeling worthy of the investment. I tried new things, adapted to new routines and learnt new practices that I would previously have never entertained. In the end I found my own source of calm in practices that suited me.

I learnt belly breathing from a relaxation therapist who advised me to breath in deeply and allow my tummy to inflate like a balloon, then pause for a minute and release. I created my own affirmation as I breathed: *'In with peace. Out with stress,'* I repeated in my mind in time with my breathing. Every time I became overwhelmed with anxiety I stopped what I was doing and used these two techniques and remarkably they worked. The more I practised them, the more I could feel the calm wash over me and my anxiety deflate from within. It was as if by magic.

When my mood was low I pushed myself to get out into nature, which I knew was a natural serotonin boost for me. I had the advantage of living in the countryside, so I had the bonus of country walks right on my doorstep. The little village I had initially hated became my salvation. Every day I went out with Bear to find new routes, not caring if I got lost, trusting my instincts and Bear's nose to find our way home. Some walks were an hour, some two or three, even. I usually ventured out at sunrise – my favourite time of day when the rest of the world remained asleep. I loved to watch the sky changing from a dusky grey to a brilliant burnt orange above a tranquil, sleeping landscape. I'd stop beside a field of sheep or a horse's paddock and watch the beginning of a new day. Grateful to witness another one.

I learnt the art of doing nothing and for once not feeling guilty for it. I allowed myself to sit and read a book – during treatment I restocked an entire bookcase. It had been taken over by nursing textbooks for five years but now I could read books of my own interest. Some were about cancer but most were about life, love and happiness. I allowed myself days to cosy up on the sofa with Bear, light my candles and burners and wrap the two of us in a blanket. With a hot cup of coffee close at hand and some chocolate, I'd read to my heart's content with no alarms set, no time restraints, no gym to run off to, no extra shifts to work. This was my time to do with as I pleased.

If it was sunny, I'd take my books outside or potter in the garden. I painted an old Belfast sink and transformed it into a quirky flower bed. I painted the outside walls and the inside too. I did whatever I pleased, whatever kept me calm. For me calmness is key now. I can't allow stress to feed back into my life and any time it does I remove myself from that situation. I have to put my own health first – physical and mental, and for me that's liberating. Learning to say no, to set boundaries, to do what is right for me without fear of what others may feel towards me. After a lifetime of undervaluing myself and my life, I realised just how valuable and precious it truly was.

In the end I learnt that spirituality doesn't come from being a diehard vegetarian or animal rights activist. It doesn't come from being a yoga fanatic or meditation guru. It comes from within. From whatever allows you to feel connected. To be still, to find peace and clarity, to slow down a little, to live in the present moment and feel comfortable with the unknown.

## Chapter 16

# -A Bear-

Halfway through chemo my yogi friend Katrina arranged for us to visit a psychic – a palm reader, located in the back of a hairdressing salon in the city centre, who had been highly recommended. I had had my palms read once before and although I had cried the entire way through, believing every word the woman had said, I went home that evening and picked through her predictions and random words with a fine-tooth comb and decided my facial expressions and short answers had led her to such readings. No, I wasn't a great believer in this kind of witchery but decided to go along for the craic anyway.

I chose to wear my jet-black wig as it was the most natural-looking one out of the bunch, and left my wedding ring at home that day, wanting to mislead the psychic and test whether this fortune teller was the real deal. Although I wasn't convinced of her ability to predict my future, I was both excited and fearful of what she might say – even if it was bullshit!

I went in first. The lights were dimmed, the usual fortune-telling trinkets were scattered about the room: a dreamcatcher here, a crystal ball there, and in the corner was a small table where the psychic gestured for me to sit. But this lady certainly didn't come across as Mystic Meg. She was more like your standard Belfast millie – Northern Irish slang for a female chav. Only this millie was older and clearly wiser – charging £30 for a 15-minute palm reading as she was.

I sat down in front of the *'psychic'* and she took my hands in hers and began tracing the lines imprinted on my skin.

*'You have a strong lifeline,'* she began.

I doubt that.

*'You're in a long-term relationship.'*

*'Yes.'* Good guess.

*'You'd like to be married.'*

Uh-uh, wrong answer. *'I'm already married.'*

*'Oh, but you're having problems in your relationship.'*

*'Perhaps.'* Ok, nice recovery.

*'You're contemplating leaving your husband.'*

*'I've thought about it, yes.'* But who hasn't?

*'He doesn't understand you.'*

No, he doesn't understand cancer.

*'You think you will be happier without him.'*

*'Erm, possibly.'* But probably not.

*'And you will be.'*

What! Really?

*'But your will also be happy with him if you go to marriage counselling.'*

*'Right, ok.'* Like that is ever going to happen.

*'You will have made your decision in six months' time.'*

I could be dead in six months' time.

*'That's when you should return for another reading.'*

Of course! So you can squeeze another £30 out of me for telling me absolutely nothing!

You can't blame me for being cynical. The palm reader hadn't exactly given me much to go on. There had been no life-changing predictions or anything significant to cling to – not as far as I could comprehend anyway. And although I was grateful she hadn't told me I was going to die, she technically isn't allowed to tell clients that.

Katrina, however, seemed to have more luck with her reading and left the hairdressers feeling optimistic rather than conned out of £30 like I did. Her reading had been career focused, which seemed fitting because she had recently started her own yoga business. My friend had also been told that she was going to be led by an Egyptian guide, which we both took to mean me after we'd supped a bottle of wine. I wasn't sure what use my guidance would be when I couldn't even guide myself but the psychic hadn't known we were together when she read our palms or of my origins, so the Egyptian guide comment intrigued us both. It's something we're still trying to figure out now.

The psychic had focused mainly on my relationship but she had also touched on a few other areas of my life – none of which involved cancer, which I found disappointing. The only prediction of interest to me was that I was apparently going to do something creative with my life.

She hadn't elaborated further on what this creative expression would be other than to say it wouldn't become my career but it would be something significant.

At the time I presumed she was referring to the mastectomy underwear I was designing, which was the only creative thing I was working on at that moment. An idea and a few designs that never went any further than my scrapbook unfortunately. But now I sense she was talking about a deeper form of creativity – maybe referring to creative writing, and one piece of writing in particular. Maybe she was referring to the piece of writing you're reading right now. Maybe that psychic wasn't such a phoney after all. Maybe she had known all along that I was going to write.

* * *

I have and always will hate group work. Having to introduce myself to a group of strangers and be forced to carry out uncomfortable icebreakers fills me with dread. I'm not really a people person, as you may have gathered. Despite having a lot of friends I am socially awkward and see myself as more of an introvert. I honestly prefer the company of animals over most human beings, which my family and friends accept, hence my strong attachment to Bear. My husband and I often joke about my love for Bear and how it exceeds my love for Graeme. He is my baby, replacing the baby I am unlikely to have now. He even acts like one.

Every morning, in a ritual that started during chemo, he lies in my arms like a human child. It's a simple routine that goes like this: I come downstairs and Bear's tail starts beating off the sofa as soon as I open the door. I say hello, ensuring I acknowledge him while making my coffee. He waits patiently knowing I'll be with him soon. Coffee in hand, I open the curtains of the double doors leading to my back garden and allow the light to fill the room, and then I join Bear on the window-facing sofa.

He flops into my arms in slow motion, still sleepy and not quite awake, and lies there until I finish my coffee; closing his eyes again and demanding tummy tickles with his paws. Every time I remove my hand he swipes it back into place. Even now, over a year later, I still get up half an hour earlier than I have to for work to ensure we have that time together. It's our time and I enjoy it as much as he does. If I'd planned my life a little better, I'd have chosen to work with animals rather than people. But, hey, there's still time yet for a career change – I hope!

Anyway, I digress. Back to hating group work. So there are a ton of different therapies available to cancer patients provided by local charities or through the NHS. After diagnosis I finally faced my fears and tried out a few of the counselling services. Some of the therapists were good and some were terrible. My first therapist, Joanne, was decent enough and I decided I liked her. But I spent the first five out of the six sessions offered to me, free on the NHS, unearthing the trauma of my childhood instead of discussing the elephant in the room, which was my cancer.

I was with Joanne throughout chemo. I saw her in between each dose, while I was losing my hair, eyebrows, eyelashes and a little piece of my mind. But despite my present hell I chose instead to talk of my previous one. In the comfort of Joanne's warm, cosy, dimly lit therapy room, sitting on fluffy purple cushions close to the ground, with the soothing scents of lavender and AromaTouch dōTERRA oils filling my nostrils and a box of scented tissues close at hand, I was finally able to open Pandora's box.

I unearthed my inner child at long last after years of burying her. I told the truth – a truth I had never spoken of with anyone. The truth about my sense of guilt surrounding my father's death and the abandonment I felt afterwards followed by my self-destructive teenage years and my shameful experiences as a young woman. My turbulent relationship with my family; the hurt and betrayal I felt after my brother, mother and grandmother walked out of my life.

My uncontrollable self-loathing and intense hatred towards my body; the episodes of self-harm, alcohol and drug abuse. And my unmerciful black dog of depression that tortured my soul. I went through boxes of those coconut-scented tissues before I revealed what I had believed all along, ever since I had heard those dreaded words *'I'm sorry, it's cancer.'* That I was a bad person and I deserved to die.

I told my truth and it was now Joanne's job to *'fix'* me, and with intense work on her side and mine, remarkably, she did just that. She rationalised my childhood experiences and negative thoughts, and finally helped me accept that my truth was untrue. After sixteen years of harbouring thoughts that my father's death was somehow my fault, I finally allowed myself to believe it wasn't. After sixteen years of believing I was a bad person, I finally accepted I was actually a good person. After feeling certain that my cancer was my fault, I finally understood that it wasn't. For a while I felt good and my mental state remained stable ... until chemo and counselling sessions with Joanne ended and I was left to my own devices again. This time I was tormented with a new trauma: my scar.

My breast care nurse referred me to a new counsellor at the end of radio after I broke down during a review appointment with her and shared the difficulty I was having accepting my mastectomy scar. But this new counsellor was no Joanne. Her room was a boring, mediocre office that lacked inviting decor and a calming atmosphere. The therapist was much older than me and a little condescending. She just stared at me when I began to cry, offering me no soft coconut tissues, and when I left feeling angrier and more upset than when I went in I decided I wouldn't be returning.

I found it difficult to explain my current dilemma with my *'ugly'* body to a woman three times my age with no understanding of my suffering. A woman who looked down her nose at me and insulted me with ridiculous advice about breathing exercises and a good night's sleep as the solution to my problems.

I knew from the moment I met that woman that I wasn't going to find the help I so desperately needed.

Since my second surgery I had struggled to look at my body without crying. I didn't allow Graeme to see my naked chest, or any of my naked body for that matter. I wore frumpy baggy clothes or polo necks that I hated to hide my prosthetic. I was paranoid that everyone knew I only had one breast, which of course anyone who knew me did know because I had shared my journey openly on social media (a part of me was now regretting my candidness). I was ashamed of the scar and the fake boob with a weird-looking nipple stuck to it, and the one remaining boob that now seemed so out of place. I felt like a freak, which was forced in my face every time I received radiotherapy; staring at the reflection of my scar and my freaky remaining boob for twenty minutes every day for three weeks. It was enough to drive me over the edge. In the midst of the war with my reflection in the mirror, I was also left searching for my missing identity – the woman I was before cancer stole her from me. I was still struggling to adapt to my new normal, and then I found art therapy.

Art was something I've always enjoyed. Although I hadn't created any artwork of my own since my teenage years, I still had a great appreciation for art and design. I stumbled upon this form of therapy in a leaflet sent to me by Action Cancer. The only problem was it happened in groups. I sent an email asking if one-to-one therapy could be accommodated (I may have told a tiny white lie claiming I had social anxiety disorder, which I probably do have undiagnosed). I assumed the answer would be a no anyway but was pleasantly surprised when the therapist replied with a yes.

I arrived for my first session the following Monday, feeling apprehensive and already regretting my email. I was sceptical of how art therapy could help my current situation and had already decided it would most likely be a complete waste of my time, just like the last counselling session. But I was there now, so I decided to see the first session through.

The charity was located, randomly, in the middle of a row of terrace houses in Belfast's city centre. After driving around aimlessly for thirty minutes in search of a parking space, I abandoned my car and entered the building with ten minutes to spare.

I checked in at reception and stood in the waiting area, already feeling too uncomfortable to sit. I glanced at the cool and funky decor. The paintings on the walls were way out of my league and I hoped I wouldn't be expected to create something of that standard. A few minutes later a lady approached me with her hand outstretched. She introduced herself as the art therapist – an older lady, I'd estimate late forties early fifties, dressed in bright orange African-print trousers with her glasses on top of her head, just how real artists wear them. I took one look at her and instantly decided I liked her. I'm going to call her Joan, to protect her privacy and because, shamefully, I don't remember her name. My bad.

Joan took me into her studio and I felt an unfamiliar twitch at the sides of my mouth. For the first time since radio finished I actually smiled – an honest and real, genuine smile, as I eagerly stared around Joan's bright, cheery workshop; soaking up the splashes of colour and intricate designs on every wall. After completing a brief assessment Joan warned me not to be too disheartened if I didn't create any art on my first day. She advised that I took a wander around the studio to get a feel for the place first, but I was instantly drawn to the desk in the far corner. I had already spotted some sketch pencils there that looked oddly familiar. As I got closer I knew they were the exact same set of watercolours my dad had bought me for one of my birthdays. The same set I still had in my drawer at home, untouched for years.

While I sketched Joan shared some of her background with me beginning with her adventures in South America. She spoke of her time living with Native American tribes and what she learnt from their traditions and ancient rituals. It sounded fascinating, strange but fascinating. These were the type of experiences I was craving now – experiences that were unique and life-changing. I had no time for the boring and mundane after cancer. Living an ordinary life was no longer for me, I had decided.

What interested me even more was to learn of Joan's discovery of her totem – a natural object or spirit animal that is meant to represent and guide you in life. Would you believe, Joan's totem is a bear? I got goosebumps. Her totem was a bear, and I was a mother to a Bear – albeit a black Labrador. But surely my choice of name and fascination with real bears wasn't a coincidence. Joan believed so to. She explained that according to Native American lore and mythology, the bear spirit bestows the gift of wholeness and completion of self in its often solitary journey. My journey with cancer had been a lonely one. In fact, my whole life had been a journey of solitude. *'The bear's rugged independence is thought to guide you to self-discovery,'* she added. And self-discovery was exactly what I was seeking. Ever since I watched Eat Pray Love I had been obsessed with finding my true self – even more so after cancer when my old self was no longer visible at all. Self-discovery was what I needed now more than anything.

I have no idea what my spirit animal is, and I'm not really sure how you find out. Google gives you a number of ways, but I doubt any of them are authentic. I would probably have to visit a Native American tribe myself to truly believe it was accurate anyway.

But if I did go to such extreme lengths, I am fairly certain I would discover that my totem is a bear.

Standing in Joan's art studio I suddenly had a feeling I had been drawn to art therapy for a reason and that I was meant to meet this artist in particular. I didn't know why, but I was sure our meeting wasn't a coincidence.

After twenty minutes or so I looked down at my creation. I had arrived that day with no intentions or expectations of what I may or may not produce. I had had no inclination of what I was going to sketch, or that my sketch was going to be of a human body – my body, to be precise. The drawing had come from within – something my mind clearly needed to express but until now hadn't been able to find a way.

I had drawn an image of my torso – no head or legs, just upper body. I had split the torso down the middle with a red dotted line. One side was a fiery red mass where my breast should have been. On the opposite side, across my remaining lonely breast, I had drawn a single wilted red rose. There were giant green flames erupting from my stomach fiercely burning away the red, angry cancerous cells that I had dotted across the torso. I had no idea where the drawing had come from other than that it was a vision I had clearly been holding in my mind. A vision of how I now saw my body. I suppose the drawing was probably quite disturbing – it was most definitely not fit for the walls outside, but as soon as I had scribbled it down on the paper I breathed a sigh of relief.

I asked Joan if I was supposed to explain my drawing to her. *'Only if you want to,'* she replied. Surprisingly, I did want to. I told her it was how I saw my body after cancer. That I imagined my body as broken, split into two sides. A red and dangerous side on the left – the cancerous side, and wilted beauty on the other – the cancer-free zone. I don't know where this description came from either, other than deep within my soul.

Joan asked me what the green fire signified. Without a moment's thought I robotically told her the fire represented the green laser beam during radiotherapy. In the image, I had drawn the green flames burning the cancer away. Maybe I had been using Bernie Siegel's visualisation techniques subconsciously all along. I don't know, but in twenty minutes I had managed to get it all off my chest, quite literally. The fear I had been holding inside up to that moment I hadn't been able to let go of.

I left Joan's art studio and cried the entire way home. I cried out of relief that I had finally discussed how cancer had destroyed my body confidence, and I cried that my body was also ruined for life. Joan had decided we would work on how I viewed my body, and had come up with a clever idea that involved us creating two moulds of my broken torso and joining them together in some fabulous artistic creation. She hoped it would bring me some level of acceptance and healing.

Our next appointment was scheduled for the following Monday. In the meantime I was sent home with homework: Joan had supplied me with my very first journal and had asked me to fill it in however I wished. Over the course of the week I could use drawings, words, magazine cuttings, anything at all to express my thoughts and feelings on that day. I could then choose to share my journal or keep it to myself. It was up to me.

That evening I wrote my first entry. It read:

## Who am I?

- I was a nurse
- I was a wife
- I was a friend
- I was a sister
- I was an aunty
- I was a daughter
- I was a woman
- I was attractive
- I was fit and healthy
- I was ambitious
- I was adventurous
- I was young
- I was free
- I was whole

## But now I am:

- Broken
- Exhausted
- Alone
- Sad
- Empty
- Ugly
- Freak
- Angry
- Different
- Fake

Beside the entry I stuck a picture of me on the beach in Cannes wearing that gorgeous orange plunging swimsuit, standing at the water's edge on that private stretch of paradise. The photo was taken three weeks after my diagnosis, after I had just received the phone call telling me that the cancer hadn't spread. In that particular photo I am posing – my arms above my head, my hands making a peace sign, and I am smiling. My body is sexy and muscular. I still have two full breasts and no ugly scars. My sun-kissed golden-brown hair is flowing freely just below my shoulders. I have gorgeous long eyelashes and my own eyebrows – not tattooed ones. I look confident and healthy and oddly happy, all things considered. I look beautiful. I stared at this image for hours and I cried. Who was that girl?

The next day I drew a sketch of me on my wedding day. I copied the image from a wedding photograph of Graeme and me that we display on a large canvas in our front room. The canvas I had taken down in disgust on numerous occasions throughout treatment because I couldn't bear to look at that girl any more. I sketched her long curly locks, her beautiful natural curves and two matching perky breasts. I shaded in the sparkle in her eyes, the laughter lines on her beautiful face and her brilliant smile. I cried as I drew the old version of me; staring at the photograph, searching for the girl I once was. Then a random thought popped into my head: what if the new me wasn't so different to the old me?

I looked at my drawing and the canvas on the wall and realised that the only things that had changed were my outward appearance. Suddenly I had a great idea for my journal. I was going to turn it into a scrapbook using photos of the old me and photos of the new me so I could compare the two women, before and now.

I printed hundreds of photos of me before and me after cancer; photos of my life before and after; photos of the people I loved before and after; photos of my Bear, my family and my friends and all the adventures we had taken together before and after cancer. I

sat at my kitchen table and I created a masterpiece. It took me three hours to fill the entire book.
Three hours to come to my final decision: I was still the same me except I was now so much more.

In the pages of that journal I was finally able to see that cancer had been my gift as well as my curse. Thanks to that unexpected gift I was now an aunty again, a sister and a daughter. I was a better wife to my husband, a better friend, a better doggy mummy and a better human being altogether. As I flicked through my creation and examined each and every photo of myself I saw so much more than just a body, whole or broken. I saw passion and creativity. I saw a great thirst for love, life and adventure. I saw everything that makes me me. I discovered that my body is just a vessel. My soul is who I really am. I saw that I was so much more than cancer! I was a survivor.

I couldn't wait to tell Joan my incredible discovery – my life-changing moment, when I discovered me again; the same me, but different. Sadly I never got the chance. In fact, I never saw my bear-loving friend again for reasons totally unrelated to cancer and because of a global pandemic known as Covid-19.

Chapter 17

# -The Rona-

I finished radiotherapy a few days after Valentine's Day, which Graeme and I had spent together at the Cancer Centre (how romantic!) while I recovered from another treatment. I used the time to plan my first solo trip to Italy; hopefully at the end of March, giving me a month to recover from radio, regain my strength and then head out to my favourite country – alone! The prospects of flying solo no longer crippled me with fear. I was a big girl now. A big girl who had just conquered cancer. I thought I could manage a journey across Italy all by myself, and I was more than ready for a new adventure. But this time I wouldn't have to please anyone else other than myself and my writing.

The idea of writing a novel first occurred to me during my steroid-fuelled insomnia in my early chemo days. Initially I'd thought about writing a blog to share my experience with breast cancer but the idea fell by the wayside when I became more engrossed in designing mastectomy underwear, completing my chemo bucket list and just trying to get through the day without having a mental breakdown. The thought of then having to sit and write about it all, forcing me to relive each experience, was just too much to handle. The trauma was too fresh at that stage.

Instead I wrote a diary – just snippets of my thoughts and feelings at the end of each evening. Some entries were more significant than others, like the time Graeme surprised me with a hack through the countryside – my very first time on a horse and one of my bucket-list challenges. The experience was a special one. He had planned the activity just after my first chemo when I still had my own hair and was just a *'normal'* girl riding a horse – except I wasn't *'normal'* and neither was the horse.

My horse was pure white and a born leader, I was told. His name was Duke and he liked to stay in front. He knew his path and all I had to do was sit up top and enjoy the view. He needed no guidance or input from me. Duke was a free spirit, and while I was with him I felt free too, just for that short moment in time.

Those special moments found their way into my diary until they didn't any more. Maybe because those freeing moments dwindled off as cancer tightened its noose around my neck. Or maybe I was too distracted with mountain climbing to write any more. Either way the diary was back-burnered, along with the mastectomy swimwear, my blog, my own podcast, a TV interview with Cancer Research, a hair-loss campaign and any other bright ideas I had to change the world. I found I didn't have time for any of it in the end, even though time was all I had.

Active treatment was a busy period of my life. I tried to cram so much living time in with my family and friends, just in case I was actually dying, that there wasn't really any time for me (or for anything else) and there certainly wasn't enough time to write a book. But writing a story wasn't just another random idea that cancer had initiated. Writing a novel had been a lifelong dream of mine since my father had told me I would write one. I still held on to that childhood vision that one day I'd hold a hard copy of my very own book. A book with my name printed across the cover. A book that would somehow change people's lives.

When radio finished I found myself standing at a crossroads unable to turn back on myself but not quite sure how to move forward either. After a few weeks of moping around the house crying continuously and only allowing myself the company of my two black dogs, I decided enough was enough. Until I knew how to move forward I would do something more useful while standing still.

I would use this period of contemplation and uncertainty to write my damn book! And where better a place to write a story than Italy.

By tying in a solo trip to Italy with writing my book I was ticking off two lifelong dreams in one go. I imagined my story coming to life in my favourite spot in Rome, Castel Sant'Angelo – a towering cylindrical building that was once used as a castle and fortress but now serves as a museum with a gorgeous outdoor coffee shop at the very top of its highest tower that provides panoramic views of Vatican City and the Pont Sant'Angelo bridge. If that didn't inspire me to write, I don't know what would. Not to mention the Italian coffee and Italian wine I could count on to keep me motivated. Yes, Italy was the perfect spot to write my first, and most likely last, memoir.

Before I headed to Italy, though, I had promised Chloe I would visit her and her two girls, Pearl and Penny. I had yet to meet Penny and barely knew Pearl, and now seemed a fitting time to finally make the effort to get to know them. Besides, I hadn't been *'home home'* in four years. I suppose I had been avoiding Blackpool, especially after the fall out with my brother, but now I looked forward to the reunion with my old friends and second families. I booked my flights without giving much thought to the news of a deadly virus wreaking havoc in China. China was thousands of miles away. Surely the virus would never find its way over here.

A week before I was due to fly the UK had their first Covid-19 case. Ok, I was a little more worried now but surely it was an isolated incident, right? In a matter of days the cases had gone up to eighteen and were steadily rising. Although Britain still seemed pretty low risk, Italy was another story. I watched in horror as my favourite country was torn apart. Thousands of people were dying. The hospitals were on their knees. Medical staff were losing their lives while trying to treat those who were infected. Morgues were overrun and bodies were piling up with nowhere to bury them.

The army was called in to remove the infected bodies before they caused even more widespread disease.

It was like something from a zombie apocalypse movie. Eventually the Italian government was forced to issue strict lockdown measures across the entire country. Italy became the worst hit European country and the new epicentre of this now global pandemic. That was until the UK overtook Italy with its number of cases and ended up with the largest death toll in the whole of Europe only weeks later.

I wisely decided against my trip to Blackpool just in time, really. Other people were still holidaying across the globe of course with no regard for the growing spread of the disease, lapping up the rapid drop in holiday prices and having a great old time. Unlike them, though, I knew I had to be sensible. I had just finished cancer treatment, my immune system was only just beginning to recover and I was more prone to infection than others. If my damaged body caught this deadly virus, I knew it would be unlikely to recover. I didn't survive cancer to be wiped out by the rona – no way, so with a heavy heart I cancelled my flights *'home home'* and put Italy off for a while too. Or maybe permanently given their current state.

Fourteen days after Italy issued their lockdown, the UK followed suit. In the blink of an eye Brits were forced to stay at home to protect themselves, their families and the NHS from Covid-19. The public's response was varied. Some panic-bought as if the world were coming to an end – you couldn't get loo roll, hand sanitiser, cleaning products, pasta or a tin of baked beans for love nor money. Supermarkets were swamped and it wasn't long before the aisles were completely emptied. It was ridiculous and it was selfish. It would be months before supermarkets could restock essential supplies, leaving some of society's most vulnerable with nothing.

Then there was the rest of the population – those who weren't in a complete state of panic and who ignored the rules entirely. These were the people who flocked to local beaches and national

parks, like they were on their summer holidays, or held lockdown parties in the streets, or worse in their houses, with no regard to the government's pleas for social distancing.
It wasn't until the death toll surged into the thousands that people got scared and heeded advice. Those who were vulnerable were sent letters telling them to shield, to not leave their homes for twelve weeks – no one in, no one out. I, of course, received a shielding letter and was devastated. So much for moving on with my life!

I had been in my own version of lockdown for the last nine months. Yes, my life was on hold long before Covid-19, and now was when I was supposed to be moving on – not forced to stay at home unable to see my family and friends; the people who had carried me through my cancer journey, my support networks, the people I needed in my life to survive pre- and post-cancer (including my brother and my nephews who had recently moved home to Northern Ireland to be close to me and our family. The two young boys had only got used to their Aunty Alex and her fun weekly visits when all of a sudden she disappeared again!

Lockdown also delayed my return to work. I had been out of work for almost a year and the longer I was off the more I feared going back. But work was definitely out of the question now – I couldn't return even if I wanted to; I had to shield and, besides, there were Covid-positive patients on my ward. There was no way I could go back to my old job. Not now – maybe not ever. To top it off I wasn't entitled to the government's eighty per cent furlough scheme, so, unlike everyone else, I wasn't paid to stay at home. I was bitter and I was angry. Fuck you, Covid-19, and fuck you, cancer!

* * *

Lockdown was a weird time for all. For some it was a time of fear and isolation with only the antics of Donald Trump and Boris

Johnson to entertain or aggravate people. For others it was a time to connect with family and friends via Zoom parties, online bake-offs and the new TikTok craze. For those infected it was a time to fight for their lives on hospital ventilators, alone and afraid.

For our frontline workers it was a time of panic and uncertainty as they faced the unknown – an unknown that threatened to wipe out their patients as well as themselves. For our children it was a time of confusion and frustration when they were pulled out of school and told they weren't allowed to see their friends any more. For me it was a time of quiet solitude. The time I had wanted to avoid but now was forced to accept. The time to reflect on my journey with cancer.

The initial four-week lockdown was extended, lasting three months in total but with further lockdowns and restrictions to follow, making 2020 everyone's worst nightmare. Despite governments' best efforts the virus was untamable and affected each person one way or another.

Mental health suffered tremendously. Anxiety and depressive symptoms heightened due to fear, isolation and limited access to services. Just like the ICU bed crisis caused by the pandemic, mental health inpatient units faced the same capacity strains. Suicide rates soared and are set to continue rising. Reports of domestic violence spiked, thought to be driven by financial stress, crowded homes, movement restrictions and reduced peer support. Alcohol and drug abuse naturally followed suit. Unemployment and redundancies skyrocketed. The whole world was falling apart, and all we could do was stay home and watch the nightmare unfold on our TV screens.

The NHS was halfway through a decade of underfunding when the pandemic hit. It was already dealing with a relatively low level of beds, dangerous staff shortages, stretched A & E and routine surgery waiting times and large cuts to social care, public health and mental health services. Although the NHS rapidly revamped their services on a large scale at the start of 2020 to release capacity for treating patients with Covid-19, all other routine care was put on hold. Thousands of patients were discharged early to free up beds, postponing planned treatment, shifting appointments to online where possible, and redeploying staff to Covid wards.

All routine hospital treatment that wasn't considered a priority or life-saving was postponed, including cancer care, so life-saving chemotherapy and radiotherapy were delayed or cancelled for thousands because it was taken as a given that the risk of a cancer patient contracting the virus outweighed the risks of postponing treatment – and it resulted in thousands of unnecessary deaths. MRIs, CT scans, vital screening and routine mammograms were all suspended, including my own. Shockingly, Macmillan are currently predicting up to 50,000 missed cancer diagnoses in the UK alone because of the pandemic. For once I felt lucky to have been told I had cancer the year previously. If I had been diagnosed during the pandemic, my circumstances may have been very different – not to mention that I would have had to face the disease alone in isolation. What an odd concept to feel lucky to have been diagnosed with cancer when I was.

The majority of my friends are nurses who were on the frontline. I naturally feared for their safety, especially when Gillian was redeployed to a Covid ward and Jenna to a Covid test centre. Our group chat, that had originally been set up to discuss my cancer, was now taken over with photos of my friends' cut faces from dreadful PPE and the daily challenges they were facing. It was hard to comfort my friends – while they were out there saving the world I was sitting at home in my bubble watching the virus wreak havoc in very shape and form and shamefully feeling bitter and resentful that my post-cancer plans weren't unfolding.

It was a bitterness that left me crippled with guilt, coupled with feeling utterly useless. I was a nurse too – or at least I used to be.

I should have been standing alongside my friends fighting the virus and helping save people's lives; not at home feeling sorry for myself as usual. But eventually I accepted that home was exactly where I was meant to be, and that I too could be useful in a very different way.

I decided that the only service I could offer the world at that time was my writing. I was sure someone somewhere, with or without cancer, would benefit from my story, so I removed all distractions, tuned myself out of Covid-19 and tuned myself in to my writing. I switched my phone to airplane mode, I stopped watching the news (that was plagued with death and disease), I stopped checking the daily death tolls online that I had been obsessing over for weeks, I stopped spending mindless hours scrolling through the same negative stories on my social media that only fuelled people's panic and despair. I turned my focus away from the apocalypse outside my front door and focused on the task at hand.

I set up my workstation at the kitchen table. The chairs were uncomfortable as hell and made my back burn even hotter, but the pain kept me alert. There was no beautiful Italian surroundings here to inspire me – just four walls, my kitchen table, coffee on tap (in my special *'like a boss'* mug that Gillian had made for me) and Bear, sitting on the sofa opposite, wondering what the hell I was doing for all those hours. I soon learnt that there is no right or wrong place to write a book. For a book to truly be authentic, the words must come from your heart not from your surroundings.

By the end of week one I had only written seven thousand words – how the hell do people actually write a book? I vented my exasperation to my husband: I wanted to tear my newly grown fluffy hair out the task was so daunting, my sentences didn't flow, the chapters were disjointed and my story didn't make any sense. But Graeme encouraged me to stick with it, and so I did. Determined this would be one thing I wouldn't quit on.

Eventually I found my rhythm. The words started to flow naturally through my fingertips. I soon had so many ideas I became overwhelmed with the number of words I had to get on paper. I wrote like a demon – like a woman possessed, often waking at 3 a.m. bright-eyed and ready to write. Unlike my late-night ventures during chemo, there was no time for sad movies on repeat or depressing soundtracks.
This time round I was a woman on a mission. A woman determined to tell my tale at long last.

Strangely I found my best ideas always came to me at 3 a.m. in the dead of night, and before the sun rose the only sounds were my fingers dancing across my keyboard. I became intrigued by this random 3 a.m. waking and so did a little digging. I found some interesting literature that suggested there's a spiritual meaning behind waking between the hours of three and five on a repeated basis. I was intrigued. Apparently waking at this time is a sign you should move toward your higher purpose in life – a time to connect with your higher self. I had never heard of the term *'higher self'* or *'higher purpose'* before cancer. I had previously employed a very black-and-white trail of thinking: anything that I couldn't see didn't exist. But cancer encouraged me to look beyond what is in plain sight and to examine myself, and life, on a much deeper level; to look within. In doing so I found my purpose, the very thing I'd spent a lifetime searching for: my purpose was to write. To write this book, in particular. The story I'm sharing with you now. The story of my ascent. A story that may one day become someone else's survival guide.

## Chapter 18

# -The Change Of Life-

A change in any situation forces us into the unknown, and people tend to fear what they are unfamiliar with. As individuals we either thrive on change or we will fall. Whether it be a change in career, a change in marital status, a change in living conditions, a change in politics or changes that affect the entire world. Whatever the circumstances of change may be, it forces us to face a new uncertainty, which can be stressful and destructive.

Although for some change is welcomed as a form of progression, unfortunately for others it is something to be resisted with stubborn determination. For me, the past year was nothing but change – all of which was completely out of my control. Between cancer and Covid, normality was certainly a thing of the past, and to be quite honest I was sick to death of change!

Previously I had used distraction to cope with or avoid change. I used drink and drugs to distract myself from my grief and family issues in my teenage years. I used the gym to avoid my marital issues after Thailand. I used the bucket list to distract myself from cancer during chemotherapy, and now I used my book as a diversion from Covid.

During lockdown I engrossed myself in my writing so deeply that I barely noticed the changes occurring outside my four walls never mind inside my own body until one morning I stood up out of bed and came crashing down to the floor. My ankles had given way from under me, snapping me back to cruel reality. The world was still in chaos – and that now included my body, as another change was forced upon me: the change of life. Almost overnight my body had aged thirty plus years. The hormone tablets I took every morning and the implant inserted in my lower belly every month had finally taken effect. My ovaries were no longer producing the essential hormones my body needed to function and my medically-induced menopause had begun.

Unfortunately the weakness and pain in my ankles were only the start of it. The lack of oestrogen in my body resulted in me losing the natural lubrication in my joints. After my first fall I quickly learnt to take my time in the mornings, shuffling my way from one piece of furniture to the next. Using them for support while gently clicking and grinding my joints awake with every painful step. The debilitation was heartbreaking. I kissed goodbye to ever returning to the gym or hiking up my favourite mountains. My body was no longer fit for it. Within a matter of months my knees followed the same pattern as my ankles, and then my fingers, and then my toes. Every joint, every muscle, every bone was affected, and there was nothing I could do about it other than take painkillers and try and persevere with my life.

My joint pain isn't entirely down to the menopause – I also have radiotherapy to thank for it. My oncologists have suggested I now have arthritis in my joints and possibly osteoporosis in my ankles (I'm waiting on scan results to confirm), but hormone therapy certainly antagonised my joints and made matters worse.

Between the pain in my back from surgery trauma and now the rest of my body shutting down, it was difficult for me to stay upbeat. Since my diagnosis I had tried to focus on the quality of my life rather than the quantity, but the quality of my life was now shattered. Hormone treatment was going against the motto I had sworn to live my life by *'to be happy in being here'* and it wasn't long before I resented the very thing that was keeping me alive. Again I contemplated whether my life was worth such agony, and I found myself facing a new and extremely difficult dilemma: do I want to live? Or do I want to exist?

Prior to experiencing menopause myself, I naively knew very little about it other than what Jim's dad had told me. I mean, it's not exactly part of the school curriculum and until recent years was rarely spoken of publicly. Of course I'd heard of hot flushes, loss of periods and increased irritability that usually occurs in women aged fifty plus, but I wasn't aware that the menopause would have such a crippling impact on all aspects of my life.

I didn't know it was possible to experience ten different moods in the space of a minute. To go from laughing, to crying, to psycho in a single heartbeat. I didn't know that the mood swings could be triggered by something completely irrational like someone crunching crisps too loudly in my ear or someone not washing the dishes. I hadn't heard of the extreme fatigue and lack of motivation that left me completely wiped out and even more irritable, or the relentless insomnia that drove me to anxious sleep-deprived sobs. I didn't know my brain would fog over in an unbreakable mist eating away at my concentration and causing me to lose the ability to string a sentence together. I didn't know menopause went way beyond hot flushes and the end of periods.

The term *'menopause belly'* was also new to me. Yes, I knew women put on weight during *'the change'* but I didn't know it all went to the midsection, creating an unpleasant overhang that left me physically repulsed. In the space of a year I'd gone from having a six-pack I was immensely proud of to a hideous muffin top. My waist vanished, none of my clothes fitted me any more and I went up three dress sizes. As if I wasn't already body conscious enough after being forced to live with only one boob for the rest of my life, I now had weight gain and cellulite to contend with as well. My body no longer felt like my own on the inside or the outside.

I begrudgingly forced myself to the doctors every month to be injected with something that was ruining my life. I held my breath and bit down hard into my lower lip when the oversized needle was inserted into my lower belly, refusing to let out even a whisper of my inner protests. Every morning I involuntarily swallowed my medication. Medication that was preventing me from having a baby. Medication that was making my life a painful misery. Medication that was ruining my marriage. Subconsciously I tried to hold off from taking the tablets for as long as possible. Sometimes it was midday or late afternoon before I opened the medication cupboard. Some days I missed them entirely. Taking my medication was the most strenuous task of the day. Unwillingly swallowing four tiny tablets was incredibly exhausting. It was a daily struggle of me against me: my mind forcing me to swallow my medication while my heart screamed, *'Please, no more!'*

The experience opened my eyes to how my patients must feel when they resist their medications. I now understood why they refuse tablets that cause them to sleep their lives away, or why they refuse medications that quieten their mind when they don't necessarily want it silenced. I now understand why they don't want to take antipsychotics that force them to pile on the pounds, or why they don't want to be force-fed nutritious supplements through a tube because they're genuinely terrified of gaining weight. I now understand my patients' resistance to treatment, resistance against the unknown, resistance against losing control of their own bodies and minds, resistance against medical staff – who postulate that they know what's best for them when they had only just met. I now understand my patients' fears, suspicions and anger. But, more importantly, I understand that their medication is necessary, just as mine is.

Sadly, necessary for my patients and myself doesn't come without sacrifice in some shape or form.

Around four months into menopause I lost my sex drive entirely. Sex become so painful I avoided it at all costs. At first I made my excuses – until excuses were no longer necessary, and my vagina's dry protests were obvious to both Graeme and me. Penetration was impossible and foreplay was no longer enjoyable. I tried a few natural lubricants (all hormone free, of course – I couldn't use standard Durex like *'normal'* people), but it wasn't long before they became a turn off too.

Eventually I withdrew from all sexual activity and physical intimacy. I didn't want to be held or cuddled. I didn't want to cosy up on the sofa in the evenings. I didn't want to be kissed or to hold hands. I just wanted to be left alone! I slowly started shutting down. My body shut down, my mind, my reproductive system and my vagina, until all that was left of me was an emotionless empty shell.

I thought Graeme would eventually leave me. Let's face it, I wasn't really giving him any reason to stick around. I was moody, irritable and no longer fulfilling my husband's needs. Although Graeme never mentioned sex, not once, I had decided he would eventually go looking for it elsewhere. I mean, how could I expect him to be celibate for the next three years whilst I was on Zoladex treatment. I figured the price for my life would, in the end, undoubtably be my marriage.

I soon found myself isolated not only from my husband, but from my family and friends also. I was uncomfortable discussing my situation with my friends. Partly because I was jealous of their *'normal'* happy lives and partly because I knew they couldn't possibly relate. Unlike cancer, which I was incredibly open about, I stayed silent when it came to menopause. I can openly admit I was ashamed and embarrassed of it.

* * *

I returned to work halfway through the pandemic, which proved to be more difficult than I anticipated. The first day I put my blues back on, I tore them off immediately in complete disgust.

Who was I kidding? I wasn't a nurse any more. My working days were exhaustingly painful due to my low mood, irrational anxiety and stubborn joint pain. Not to mention the trauma response it evoked every time I drove past the Cancer Centre on my way in.

I then started to believe my work colleagues hated me and were talking about me behind my back without any evidence of this irrational belief other than I was just certain of it. I found myself hiding in back offices trying to catch a breath, and spending the majority of my day fighting back tears. My mind was tortured with negative thoughts. Even when I was sleeping I couldn't escape my own negativity. Every night I dreamt the same dream: I was trapped in work, all the doors were locked and I couldn't escape. Both patients and staff were pointing at my fake boob, shouting *'freak'* at me, laughing and sneering in my face. I woke most nights in a sweaty breathless panic counting down the dreaded hours until another torturous working day.

I started having panic attacks, usually as I drove in or out of work. They got that bad that I found my chest tightening and I struggled to get a breath, forcing me to pull the car over and carry out my belly breathing techniques before I could drive on. On my days off I moped around in my jammies scrolling through endless job sites, searching for a way out, looking for any occupation that wasn't nursing. But there was nothing that appealed to me. I wished I didn't have to work at all but at twenty-nine retiring isn't an option!

The stress I was under in work naturally projected into my home life – a stress that I had sworn to avoid. After another miserable ten-hour shift I arrived home to an untidy kitchen and Bear still waiting for his daily walk. Pre-menopause I may have let this slide, but now that I was a hormonal mess an untidy kitchen was enough to send me into a fit of rage. Bearing in mind I now suffered with severe fatigue and had gone back to almost full-time hours while dealing with crippling anxiety and facing the pressures of working in a clinical setting that put me at greater risk of catching Covid-19 when I was supposed to be shielding, of course an untidy kitchen and un-walked dog was enough to send me over the edge. A full-blown row erupted in my home that evening. Yes, I may have overreacted by telling my husband to move out because of some unwashed dishes, but I hadn't expected the situation to escalate as far as it did.

Graeme had naturally lost the rag with me and stormed upstairs. After a short cooling-off period I followed him, believing we would laugh this silly row off as we had all the others, and that all would be forgiven. But this time when I entered our bedroom the atmosphere was different. You could cut the tension with a knife and my husband's face was livid. I cautiously sat on the edge of the bed and let my husband speak for a change. He stared at the wall, unable to make eye contact with me, his face turning from anger to sorrow. *'I miss my wife, Alex, and I don't know how to get her back.'*

I sat in stunned silence. I suppose I hadn't given much thought to how my situation affected Graeme. I had been so preoccupied with how cancer affected me, I had selfishly believed I was the only victim in this marriage. I now realised cancer hadn't just robbed me of my former self, it had also robbed my husband of his former wife too. Neither of us had signed up to this on that cliff in Sorrento and it was unfair on both of us. It wasn't just *'why me?',* it was *'why us?'.*

Graeme told me how ignored he felt. How I barely acknowledged him any more. How I was emotionless around him and how I seemed to have lost all passion for him and for my life. I knew I had begrudgingly accepted my fate and detached myself from pretty much everything and everyone I loved, but I hadn't realised my fate didn't need to destroy my husband's. Or maybe I had but I didn't want to accept it. Graeme still had a bright and healthy future ahead of him, after all. A future that would look much brighter and happier if I and my cancer were no longer a part of it. Maybe it would be kinder to let my husband go? Maybe facing the future alone would be the best solution for both of us?

*'What if we separate and just remain friends,'* I suggested.

*'I can't do that, Alex. It's all or nothing, you know that.'*

*'I don't want you to stick around out of guilt because I had cancer,'* I answered.

*'If that was the case, I'd have left long ago.'*

The room fell silent.

I don't want to lose you, Graeme. But I don't know how to keep you either.

* * *

After another sleepless night I got up early to take Bear for a long walk and clear my head. Graeme and I had agreed to try and work on things, but we both agreed this would be the last time we would. Divorce was now a very real possibility and I knew something drastic needed to change, although I still felt it was my husband who needed to make all the changes not me. I threw on my oversized coat, plugged my headphones in, squeezed my swollen achy ankles into my walking boots and searched for a podcast.

The podcast world was still relatively new to me. Prior to cancer I wouldn't have thought to tune in – I'd always preferred books or the internet as my go-to sources of information. But since diagnosis I had found them educating, interesting and honest. There was no bullshit on the shows I listened to. Just real people sharing real experiences. I devoured books throughout my treatment and will always have a passion for reading, but it was nice to have a variety of sources of information, especially when I needed to give my eyes and head a rest and just listen.

I have two favourite shows I listen to religiously. The first one is The Melissa Ambrosini Show, where Melissa interviews a series of pretty cool and inspiring thought leaders from around the globe and they describe how they made epic changes in their lives. Each interview has a different focus and Melissa covers a huge variety of content. It's impossible not to learn something new and valuable during each episode. My second is You, Me and the Big C – a cancer-focused podcast led by a group of individuals who either had, still have cancer or have lost a loved one with cancer. This is obviously super close to home for me and although upsetting at times is always relatable.

Both podcasts helped me enormously through my cancer and healing journey and I needed help again, so I typed *'menopause'* into the search bar and hoped to find another useful podcast to add to my toolbox. The top result was titled Menopause: The Good, The Bad & The Downright Sweaty. I scrolled through the episodes and found exactly what I was looking for: *'Menopause and Relationships Part. 1.'*

As I walked with Bear along the familiar country lanes I found myself relating to everything the two relatively young presenters were discussing: how these women both had experienced medically-induced menopause for reasons other than cancer; how they had distanced themselves from their partners; how they both struggled with physical intimacy; how they had suffered with depression, suicidal thoughts and severe anxiety; how they withdrew from their friends and family; how they struggled with constant irritability, hot flushes and panic attacks. I found myself unconsciously nodding my head in agreement with it all!

I extended my walk a little longer, desperate to hear more despite the heavy rain breaking through the trees. I moved on to the next episode: *'Menopause and Relationships: A man's perspective.'* This time it was the husbands' or partners' turn to share.

Surprisingly, hearing the men's experience of menopause saddened me even more than the women's version had. Would you believe the two men used the exact words Graeme had used to describe me – empty, blank and vacant? They also spoke of how they struggled with feeling unwanted and useless. Poor them and poor Graeme. On a brighter note, the podcast did finish with some useful tips on how both couples learnt to adjust in their very different situations, which ultimately made all the difference in helping them remain together. Ok, there's still hope for us yet, then. They concluded that the reason behind their relationships' success was down to one key principle: education.

I realised that Graeme and I had never fully prepared for *'the change.'* Neither of us had researched it or sought advice on how to handle the side effects of menopause. We'd gone into this battle practically blind with a useless medication leaflet (that Jim's dad had given us months ago) as our only weapon. As Bear and I tottered up the drive in a weary, muddy mess, I accepted it wasn't Graeme alone who needed to change – it was both of us, and the way to move forward was by arming ourselves with knowledge and educating ourselves on the menopause.

The following Friday evening I arranged a date night. Bearing in mind Belfast was back in another mini lockdown and my choice of location was therefore limited, I worked it in my favour. I decided we would go for a drive to Tim Hortons drive-through. Customers weren't permitted to sit in, which again suited me better. A French vanilla latte to go would work perfectly. I knew Graeme would pooh-pooh the idea immediately if I told him what I had planned, so I kept it a surprise and successfully managed to trick my husband into spending his Friday evening sitting in Tim Hortons car park with a coffee, a cup of tea and some bite-sized donuts listening to women's problems over the car's sound system. After his initial mortification, even he could admit the date was a success. Graeme related to the men on the podcast just as I had related to the women.

I watched as light-bulb moments fired off in both our heads like a faulty set of Christmas tree lights: so that's the reason I can't remember anything any more! So that's the reason she can't bear to be touched! With understanding came acceptance and a formulated plan on how we could proceed as a couple. The first change we decided to make, right there and then in Tim Hortons car park, was to be kinder to each other.

Over the next few months I worked hard on being nicer to my husband. I held my tongue and paused before starting unnecessary arguments. I apologised on the few occasions I didn't manage to keep my mouth shut, and my apologies were accepted. I made small changes to ensure Graeme felt acknowledged, like stopping at the garage on my way home to buy him his favourite chocolate or remembering to text him when I was at work to ask how his day was going or sending him funny photos of Bear with his tongue hanging out to make him laugh. I wanted to show my husband that I still loved him and wanted him because I did love him, more than anything (except Bear, of course), and I understood he needed to feel my love, not just hear it. If I could only display my affection with a brief cuddle on the sofa in the evening or by placing my hand on top of his in the car or giving him a gentle kiss goodnight, for him that was enough.

Graeme worked on being nicer too. He learnt to be more patient with me and hold his tongue if I snapped. He too apologised on the few occasions he didn't, and his apology was accepted. He understood my obsession over household chores, and we came up with a system that ensured he helped with the workload. He made more time for me to encourage me to do things I previously enjoyed, but to do them together this time round and at a much slower pace. He was more considerate, even if it was only making me a cup of coffee in the mornings or occasionally cooking dinner or running me a hot bath after work. The small gestures made a difference. Our passion between the sheets may have been replaced with tear-stained cuddles instead on the nights when it was all too much for both of us, but I finally quit masking my pain from him.

His reassurance was comforting instead of empty like before because he finally understood how I felt, and for me that was enough.

I am no marriage expert but I certainly know this. In only three short years of marriage ours has faced more turmoil and uncertainty than most marriages sustain in a lifetime, and yet we are still together and still going strong. Our marriage isn't a typical one, but then it never really was. We come from completely opposite worlds – a bit like my own parents did. Me from a busy English seaside town; him a country boy born and bred. Me the ASBO teenager; him the ideal pupil. Me an adrenaline junkie; him cautious and always by the book. Him a home bird, whereas I'm always looking for the next adventure. Yet despite our differences we complement each other. We love each other, and we can't be apart from one another. For me it doesn't get much better than that.

# Chapter 19

# -I Did It-

I had made it through another Christmas. Like many people in the cancer community, I find Christmas is a significant milestone; one that many of us cannot help but fear may be our last. However, this Christmas, I didn't have the same morbid feelings that had plagued my previous one. Instead I was hopeful.

This Christmas period had been a strange one – even stranger than the last, which was largely spent in hospital fighting for my life. This year the festive holidays were spent in a very different form of isolation, another lockdown. Graeme and I had agreed to spend Christmas with my family this year, at my brother's new house. We bent the rules ever so slightly and mixed three households, inviting my mum and her husband too. It was our first family Christmas since my father had passed – with a few additional members and two very excited little boys. My nephews made Christmas for us all, and I knew our family was one of the lucky ones getting to spend the day together.

There would be many spending Christmas alone – grandparents in nursing homes unable to receive visitors; stranded lorry drivers stuck at European borders unable to make it home for Christmas; thousands in hospital, unsure if they would live to see another one, alongside burnt-out medical staff who sacrificed their family Christmas dinner to nurse the diseased and dying, risking their own lives in the process; people forced into isolation over Christmas and New Year after being in close contact with the virus, many of who lived alone. Not to mention the hundreds of children who would wake up to no presents under the tree this year after their parents had lost their jobs. It was a bleak Christmas for many and I thought of all those people, the old and the young, as I stared at our Christmas feast laid before me, and my family gathered around it, thanking the heavens that we were the lucky ones.

With Christmas being a quiet one, and an even quieter New Year looming, I decided to make New Year's Day a day to remember – kicking the year off as I meant to go on, on a high. Despite the country suffering a depressing low, I was determined Graeme and I would make the day eventful – after all, I may not live to see another one myself!

Luckily for us, there had been a bout of cold weather over the holidays leaving higher ground blanketed in fresh clean snow. My social media had become plastered with photos of the Mourne Mountains covered in the fluffy white stuff and I was itching to take some shots of my own. So I convinced Graeme to join me in toasting the New Year with a cup of hot coffee at the top of those snowy mountains and a view of the first sunrise of 2021. Graeme was surprisingly game for the idea and had the head torches in the backpacks at the ready. And that's why, on New Year's Eve, my husband and I were tucked up and fast asleep by ten, completely sober (a first), with our alarms set for 3.30 a.m.

* * *

I had first reattempted the Mourne Mountains exactly one year previous. Again, on New Year's Day, with Gillian and her friend Gillian. I had stupidly chosen to climb the highest mountain in the region, Slieve Donard. It was a month after my second surgery and my body was still in a lot of pain. I had also been rendered pretty much immobile after having my lymph nodes removed, and for the previous month had done very little physical activity. I knew the journey to the top would be a difficult one but it never crossed my mind that I may not be able to complete it. I had climbed it during chemotherapy, and surely my body was in a worse state back then than it was now. Turns out it wasn't.

The trek to Donard's summit begins in a forest. The trail follows a river and gradually begins to climb more steeply through the woodland before entering a valley between two of the highest peaks of the Mournes. On arrival at the saddle-shaped dip between the two peaks, you then turn left for the final and exceptionally steep ascent to the top, to the summit, which stands 848m above sea level and is the highest point in Northern Ireland. The previous year I only just made it through the forest. We were no more than thirty minutes into the trek when I had to ask my friends to stop while I sat defeated by a large oak tree and tried to catch my breath. My chest was heaving – it had never been the same since that infection at the end of chemo. As I struggled to get air into my lungs, I started to panic, which only made the situation worse. *'It's ok, Alex, we don't have to go any further,'* Gillian reassured me. But we did. I was not a quitter.

I forced myself to the saddle before I caved in to defeat, knowing there was no way my lungs would sustain that final steep ascent. We ate our picnic in silence by the shelter of the Mourne Wall. I was devastated. I had climbed this mountain over and over during my Everest training without batting an eyelid. Flip, I had practically run up and down it! I had continued to climb it during chemo without any real difficulty. Although it exhausted me now, my body had never failed to carry me to the top. Not until that day.

Back in the comfort of my own home I let the tears fall just as I knew they would. Today was the first day cancer had beaten me – the first day it had won, and I was beyond devastated. I wondered if I would ever be able to do the things I loved again. Would I ever be able to do the things I enjoyed? Would I ever stand on the tops of mountains again?

My second attempt ended the same way as the first – I was at the saddle again before I was beaten and had to climb back down; my frustration heightening with yet another defeat. My third attempt I did alone. My first ever solo hike – just me and Bear, of course. Although arguably Bear only made it more difficult because he was badly behaved throughout the entire hike. The mountains tend to make him a little crazy as he loves them as much as I do. I climbed much slower than usual, taking my time, taking it easy. Today was the day I'd reach the summit. I was sure of it. Bear and I stopped at the saddle – the usual picnic spot, and ate our lunch: me, my sandwiches, and him his gravy bones. I sat for a while, daunted by the mighty hill to the left of me, but eventually I stood and began my final ascent with Bear beside me and with sheer determination. I dragged my miserable body to the top of that mountain, refusing to let cancer beat me any more!

* * *

One year later, on another New Year's Day, Graeme and I left the house at 4 a.m. sharp. It was an hour and a half drive and I wanted to ensure we made it to the summit before sunrise at half eight. We drove down the deserted motorways hoping to avoid police vehicles during curfew. The fine if we were caught was £1,000. Thankfully we saw no lights except our own and dodged the hefty bill.

Graeme drove and, as usual, controlled the music from his mobile phone. After half an hour or so of sleepy silence, he turned to me. *'I've wanted to play this song to you for a while now but was waiting for something special. Today seems fitting enough.'* He can be so sentimental at times. I braced myself and listened, already knowing this would be emotional. He played *'Wind Beneath My Wings'* by Bette Midler. We managed to get to the chorus before I burst into tears, and so did he. It was the first time my husband had acknowledged my struggles as well as my strengths. Unable to say the words himself, he played them through the song. I took his hand in mine and stared out the window, lost in my own unspoken words for the rest of the journey.

We arrived at five thirty, parked up, threw our gear on our backs and began our climb. We were the first ones on the mountain that morning. It was pitch-black, with only the moonlight and our head torches to guide the way. A dark silhouette of the mountain peaks loomed before us blanketed in silver stars. It was mesmerising. In fact, I couldn't take my eyes of it.

We couldn't tell if there was snow on the peaks, not yet – it was still too dark, but I was praying there was. For now I had to focus on the difficult task at hand: navigating a mountain in the dark. Having climbed this mountain a handful of times, I knew the way better than my husband, so I stayed out in front.

I had chosen to climb Slieve Binnian, a half-day route that summits one of the seven highest peaks in the Mournes. The trail is usually easy enough to navigate, and if in doubt you can always follow the crowd as it's one of the more popular hikes because of its breathtaking views. But like I said, we were the only ones there in the dark, so following wasn't an option. The trail isn't so much a path but rather a narrow area of flatter ground, that has been repeatedly walked on, snaking its way up the mountain face. Luckily there's always the Mourne Wall to follow – an ancient wall built in 1904 that stretches a whopping twenty-two miles across the mountain region and includes fifteen of its peaks. *'Our next challenge,'* I said, pointing it out to Graeme.

For the first half hour or so the terrain was relatively clear with very little ice. Easy enough, I naively thought, until we reached the start of the rocky ascent, which turned out to be treacherous. The rocks were covered in solid ice and my feet were slipping and sliding all over the show. The ice cracked beneath my boots with every terrifying step. This is it, this is how I'm going to die, I thought to myself. My fear of falling was somewhat justified because I'm more at risk of fractures and breaks than Joe Bloggs after completing radiotherapy, which I had to continuously remind my husband who was starting to lose patience with me. But no matter how I tried, it was impossible to get a grip on the ice. I ended up on my hands and knees in some of the trickier spots to avoid seriously injuring myself.

The black sky was quickly turning a brilliant purple but we were only halfway up. It was now a race against time, and I was slowing us down. I turned to see a trail of head torches behind us catching up, urging me to speed up. My competitive side kicked in – I didn't want to be overtaken, but my legs were heavy and exhausted, my arms were burning from clinging onto the wall so tightly, using it for leverage. Three couples passed me and I was growing ever more frustrated knowing that in my pre-cancer days I'd have beaten every one of them to the summit. But still I climbed.

Finally the ice turned to white fluffy snow (thankfully much easier to walk on), and Graeme and I were able to pick up the pace – full steam ahead. We made it to the top with only ten minutes to spare. A mist had unfortunately crept up on the mountaintop making visibility exceptionally poor. You could see nothing, and I prayed it would clear in time for sunrise. While we waited we took shelter behind an icy rock, drinking our hot tea and coffee and wishing fellow hikers a happy New Year. It was a heart-warming experience to be part of a group of strangers gathered in the freezing snow to watch the first sunrise of 2021.

Ten minutes passed and my hands started trembling with the cold; my gloves insufficient in sub-zero temperatures. I knew I wouldn't be able to wait much longer. When suddenly, low and behold, the mist cleared and the sun rose in a blaze of orange and yellow; shining upon the mountain summit and turning the snow into a bed of glittery diamonds. It was one of the most breathtaking sights I have ever witnessed – and I've seen some wonders in my time. This, however, was something else. I wished we could stay longer but my body temperature was plummeting and I was starting to convulse. I urged Graeme to begin our descent down the opposite, less treacherous, side of the mountain. Once we had made sufficient ground and I had warmed a little, we stopped so Graeme could fly his drone. The snow here was still fresh and untouched; our footprints the only markings on an otherwise blanket of pearly white. The snowy peaks of the surrounding mountaintops were in full view, and this was the perfect spot for some video footage.

Later that evening, in front of our blazing fire and with a scalding cup of coffee in hand, Graeme edited the drone footage and played me the video. I couldn't stop watching it over and over. It was hypnotic. I watched myself slipping, sliding and smiling up that snow-drizzled mountain and felt as though I was seeing myself for the first time. In that picturesque video, made by my talented husband, I saw the beneficiary of cancer, not the victim.

I had been given a gift – a gift that so many are heartbreakingly deprived of – the gift of time, extra time. Time to spend with my husband, family, friends and most importantly my fur baby Bear. Every minute of every day is a gift that I could have otherwise lost. Every morning when I wake I make a point of saying thank you – thank you is always the first words to leave my lips. Some days I repeat it over and over and some days I whisper it only once. But I always make sure I say it and truly mean it. No matter how difficult my day ahead may be, I am still thankful to live another one regardless.

My enormous gratitude for my life would never have existed if I hadn't been forced to face my own mortality. I watched my snowy mountain ascent unfold on our TV screen and saw my journey with cancer in every step of it. A journey I was now grateful for. An epic quest that had led me to myself and the life I was meant to live – a whole one full of love, life, laughter and adventure. I had climbed my very own Everest in the end; an exhausting, heartbreaking cancerous Everest, and I did it with grace, honesty, integrity and superhuman strength. A strength I would have otherwise never known I possessed. I handled it like a true champion. Never letting it wear me down. Never letting it win. No matter how much it threatened me, I remained resilient. Even in the pits of my own abyss I never gave up. Even when I was sure it was the end of the trail for me, I kept climbing, I kept fighting and I kept on with my ascent. Because on the top of those mountains, where the sky is my only limit, I am at peace. Supported and grounded by the earth beneath my feet, free to soak in the beauty of my surroundings, to feel the warmth of the sun on my bare skin, to admire the stunning views below me and the beauty of another sunrise above me. Each one reminding me of my new beginning, my second chance at life. Up there where the air is pure and crisp, I breathe freely without face masks, without fear, without Covid-19, without cancer. Such worries don't exist at those heights for my mind is now as sturdy as the mountains I stand upon. No longer plagued by mental ill health or by a deadly disease, up there at the top of my ascent I am finally free!

* * *

The evening after our moonlit hike, as I rested my exhausted body in our supersized bed, I pulled out my little black journal from my bedside drawer, the journal that my quirky, fellow bear-loving art therapist had given me months ago, and took another look through the pictures I had filled it with. In that same drawer I keep a handful of photos that mean something to me. Not photos of people, but photos of places. Places I wish to visit before I die. Among them was a shot of Mount Everest. I took the photo of the highest mountain on earth in my hands and stuck it on the journal's final page. Underneath I wrote the words: I DID IT.

I did it. I had survived my own Everest and I had benefited from my ascent! As heartbreaking as cancer was, my journey with it allowed me to heal what had long been broken. It healed me. Cancer gifted me with the peace and clarity I had been longing for my whole life. It gave me joy in ways I never could have imagined. It reunited me with my family and solidified friendships that will last for eternity. It opened doors to new opportunities that I would otherwise never have experienced (including the opportunity to live as a patient to become a better nurse). As well as giving me the chance to meet some incredible and inspiring people in a community I am welcomed into and privileged to be part of. A community of survivors who also have a story to tell. Stories that I learnt and grew from.

Finally, cancer gifted me with a new form of creative expression – writing. Cancer had led me to my purpose at long last. My purpose was to write, and to write this story in particular. A personal and emotional memoir of the most difficult and elevating ascent of my life. A story of pain, loss and suffering but also hope, joy and light. A story that transformed me and my life as I wrote it. A story that allowed me to find peace and closure at long last. My story was my gift. A gift that I now pass on to you and whoever else needs to read it.

For months my writing had been at a stalemate. I had been stuck on my final chapter for what felt like infinity, waiting on a miracle to finish with. Perhaps a miracle baby or a dream trip to Italy, India and Bali, a new and marvellous career. Whatever it was, I wanted it to be spectacular. But on the summit of that freezing mountain, in the early hours of that icy-cold New Year morning, I came to an important realisation: my life was the greatest miracle I could ever finish my story on. I didn't need to wait for something extraordinary to happen because my second chance at life was already just that – extraordinary. At long last my story was complete and with it my cancer journey (for now, at least) has come to an end. It has taken me a full year, a year of recovering and a year of writing, to fully grasp the concept of ringing the cancer bell and the poem written above it:

*Ring this bell*
*Three times well*
*Its toll to clearly say*
*My treatment is done*
*This course is run*
*And I am on my way!*

**(Inspired by Emma Payton and Maria Watt)**

Although I had physically rung the bell that day in the Cancer Centre at the end of active treatment with my family, friends and fellow cancer patients cheering me on, mentally I am only hearing its chimes now. One year later and I can finally say, *'I am on my way.'*

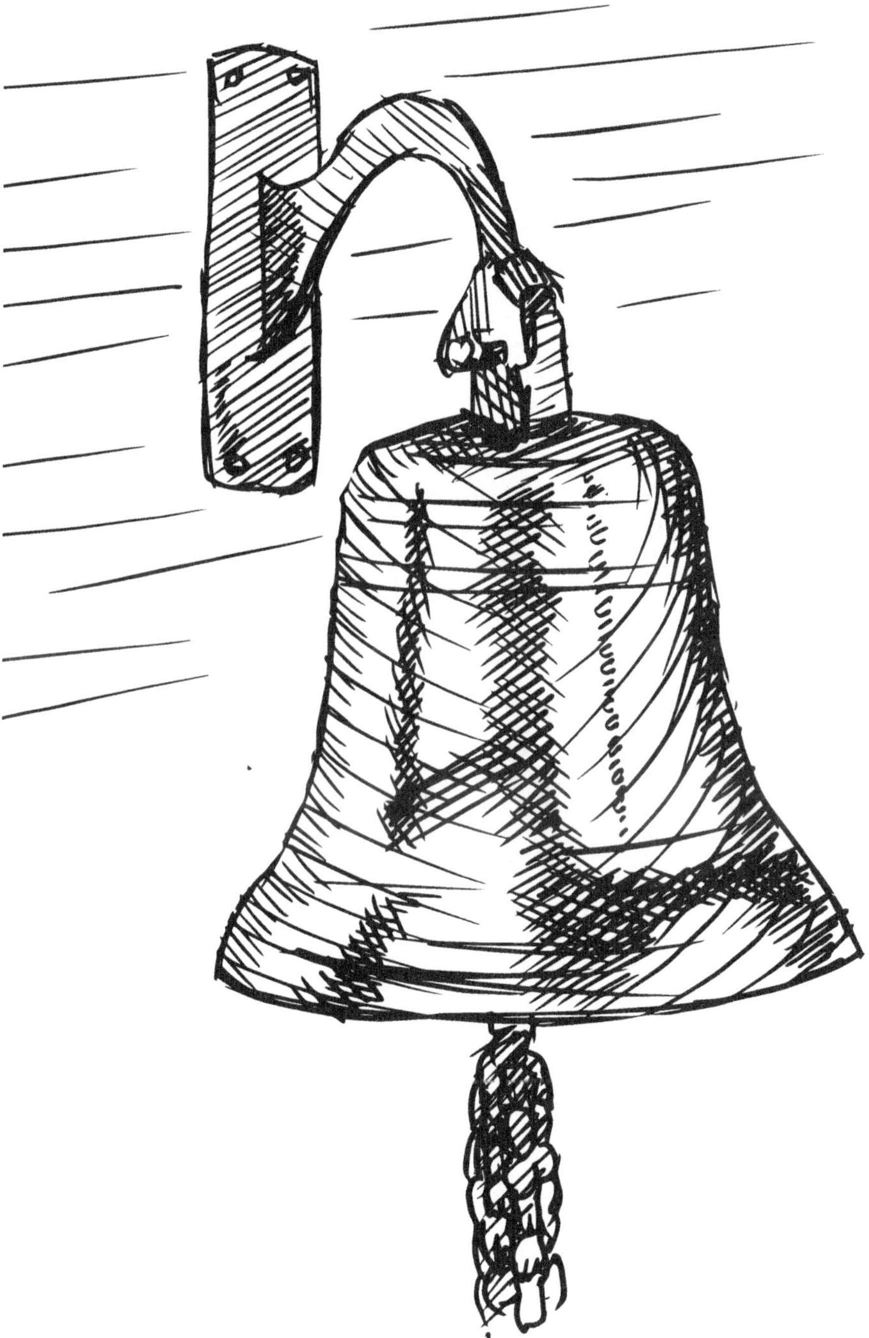

Printed in Great Britain
by Amazon

65787230R00119